Bring Mati Home

Bring Mati Home

THE TRUE STORY OF A FATHER'S SEARCH FOR HIS ABDUCTED SON IN BANGLADESH

· · ·

Tyler Wood

ISBN: 1545339554
ISBN 13: 9781545339558
Library of Congress Control Number: 2017903927
CreateSpace Independent Publishing Platform
North Charleston, South Carolina

Foreward

• • •

THE VALUE OF CLOSE FRIENDS and a support network has been critical in the success of rescuing my son. Unfortunately, parental child abductions happen everyday. I would like to offer this forward as a road map in the effort to help those that may find themselves or a loved one in the unfortunate situation I was in just a few years ago.

Your local law enforcement, FBI, and U.S. State Department are always the first step in reporting a child abduction. The US State Department has a Children's Issues service dedicated to this very real problem that thousands of families are dealing with.

Additionally, mediation and other strategies should be considered as you map out your rescue attempt. The IECC, http://www.childabduction. com, is an organization that specializes in repatriation and recovery of internationally abducted children. They have mediators and legal connections around the world with a very high success rate. Their hotline can be reached 24 hours a day, 7 days a week: +31-6-51566221

Another direction that should be considered and consulted with is Naples Security Solutions. http://naplessecuritysolutions.com. The managing partners have military and secret service backgrounds that may be necessary in the most critical of circumstances. Michael Perl and Chris Knott are the managing partners and personal friends:

Michael Perl directs executive security consulting and protection services, oversees corporate and criminal investigations, and heads a data forensic services team. Over the course of more than a decade in the U.S. Secret Service, Michael has planned and executed security operations in more than 25 countries, identifying and mitigating threats and vulnerabilities to sitting and former Presidents of the United States. Michael provided physical protection and conducted protective advance work both domestically and internationally, often in hostile environments such as the Middle East and South America. Michael served with the U.S. Secret Service Special Operations Division and was assigned to the elite Hazardous Agent Mitigation and Medical Extrication and Rescue Team (HAMMER).

Chris Knott leads corporate & special event security divisions, and domestic, matrimonial & child custody security and investigative services, offering consultations and assistance with investigations, event security planning, and protection. Prior to entering the corporate world, Chris spent almost a decade as a Naval intelligence officer serving in combat missions in Bosnia, Iraq and Afghanistan and quickly rose to the rank of First Class Petty Officer (E-6). During that time, he supported multiple Navy SEAL teams and held the highest national security clearance, earned five Navy and Marine Corps Achievement Medals and 28 Letters of Commendation.

Acknowledgements

• • •

This book would not be possible without the spiritual encouragement and belief of my parents, Yvonne & Woody Wood, and my inner circle of support, Trent Young, Amanda Erwin, Joe Anthony, Nick & Laura Garulay, Onur Haytac, and Matthew Kelley, as well as the guidance of Susan Boucek for getting this work going in the right direction.

The rescue, itself, would never have happened without the emotional, financial, and logistical support of so many old friends and new, including many people encountered along the way at precisely the right juncture. Timing is everything, and I want to specifically mention the help I had formulating my mediation and all the intercultural navigators on Mati's path to freedom, including the generous contributions of my GoFundMe. com crowd-funding campaign: Nick and Laura Garulay, Onur Haytac, Ross and Rani Howard, Monica Pollitt, Lynn Mount, Joe Anthony, Shelley McKernan, Amanda Erwin, Charlotte Luer, Derek and Liz Robertson, Annette Bennett, Ryan Bladen, Michael Guthrie, Scott Quinn, Rob Angelica, Linda Cusumano, Susan Mason, Edlyn Colon, Thea Mason, Jungwon Kim, Danna Hessey, Pat Macdonald, Al and Sande Maggiacomo, Lu Doan, Corey Stranger, Kate McEleney, Kim Rymer, Chadd Phipps, Cesar Alsina, Isabela Omeara and several anonymous donors.

A special thanks to Hans and Zahid, without whom I would have never been able to accomplish the monumental task of assembling my Bangladeshi legal team and logistical coordination, many of whom were friends whose names I have changed for their own protection. To my Naples legal team, Paul and Amanda Rocuant, mediator Holly Chernoff, and Ted Hudgins, thank you for your patience and astute guidance.

Deepest gratitude, as well, to the US State Department and their parental support team, along with FBI and Collier County Florida's local law enforcement agencies.

Steps to Stopping an Abduction in Progress

· · ·

**24 Hours a day, contact us at 1-888-407-4747 or
via e-mail at PreventAbduction1@state.gov**

IF YOU HAVE REASON TO believe that your child is in the process of being abducted by a parent, legal guardian, or someone acting on their behalf, there are steps that can be taken to prevent the abduction. Immediate steps you can take include:

CONTACT THE OFFICE OF CHILDREN'S ISSUES, PREVENTION BRANCH AT 1-888-407-4747

* **OBTAIN A COURT ORDER:** A court order is vital to preventing the departure of a child. You can retain an attorney to discuss your options. Law enforcement may not be able to act unless there is a court order that prohibits the child's travel outside of the United States. Court orders preventing the removal of the minor child from the court's jurisdiction, the state, or the country will give law enforcement more authority to prevent abduction. For information regarding prevention under the International Child Abduction Prevention and Return Act visit here and also review our page titled Law and Regulations.

- **CONTACT LAW ENFORCEMENT:** Contact law enforcement immediately and inform them of any court orders and the potential for international parental child abduction. Request that law enforcement enter information about your child as missing person in the National Crime Information Center (NCIC) as soon as possible, so that your state's troopers or highway patrol can widen the search for your child. When working with any law enforcement official ask for the officer's full name, e-mail, fax number, direct phone number, a dispatch line with 24 hour coverage, and backup officer.

- **CONTACT AIRPORT POLICE AND THE AIRLINES:** Contact the airlines and airport law enforcement that is stationed at the departing airport, if known. Because the United States has no exit controls, abductions can only be prevented if the appropriate authorities at ports of exit are made aware of courts orders that prohibit travel prior to departure. When contacting airlines, ask to speak with an airline corporate security officer, explain the situation, be ready to prove you have a parental relationship to the child, and ask if there is a reservation under your child's name. This can help mobilize efforts to stop child abductions.

The International Child Abduction Prevention and Return Act (ICAPRA), signed into law on August 8, 2014, contains provisions that increase the Department's annual reporting requirements. Each year, the Department will submit an Annual Report on International Parental Child Abduction to Congress by April 30. Additionally, the Department will submit a subsequent report to Congress on the actions taken towards those countries determined to have been engaged in a pattern of noncompliance in the Annual Report on International Parental Child Abduction.

Prior to 2015, as formerly required under 42 U.S.C § 11611, the Department published an annual report on countries that did not comply with their treaty obligations under the 1980 Hague Convention on the Civil Aspects of International Parental Child Abduction (Convention).

The previous compliance report identified countries that were not compliant with the Convention, showed patterns of noncompliance with the Convention, and had Convention enforcement concerns. The report listed cases that remained open and active for 18 months or more after the Convention application was filed.

* A detailed custody order and good legal advice can go a long way in protecting your parental rights.
* Detailed custody orders include special provisions on the custody decree such as specifying the beginning and end dates of visits; relocation restrictions; supervised visitation for the potential taking parent; requiring the court's approval to take the child out of the state or country; and asking for the court or a neutral third party to hold passports.
* Consult your attorney about the drawbacks to joint-custody orders in parental abduction cases, if ordered. Ensure that you clearly specify the child's residential arrangements at all times.
* Do not ignore any abduction threat. Notify police and give them copies of any restraining order on your ex-spouse. You may also request restricted locations for visitation rights if you can prove potential harm to your child.
* Be on the alert for sudden changes in the other parent's life. Changes, such as quitting a job, selling a home, or closing a bank account, may be signs that the parent may be planning to leave the country.
* Don't delay action if you think your child has been taken by the other parent. Make sure that if your child is abducted, the police take a detailed report and that your child is entered into the FBI's National Crime Information Center (NCIC) system right away (a warrant is not required).
* Be aware that if one parent is a citizen of another country, your child may have dual nationality. Contact the embassy of that country and inquire about their passport requirements for minors.

Frequently Asked Questions

• • •

GENERAL QUESTIONS

What do I do if my child has been taken and I don't know where he/ she is?

You should contact the Department of State's Office of Children's Issues by phone at 1-888-407-4747 or by e-mail at PreventAbduction1@state.gov if you think a child has been abducted overseas. You should also start working with law enforcement as early as possible and keep a written record of the people and agencies you have contacted as well as their telephone numbers and relevant contact information. Local police can work with you to have your child's name entered into the National Crime Information Center (NCIC), to assist in searching for your child. If you believe your child has already been taken out of state, you should also notify the nearest FBI field office. Be advised that some law enforcement agencies may be less responsive if there is no court order. If you have difficulty getting local law enforcement to focus on the search for your child, contact the National Center for Missing and Exploited Children's 24-hour hotline at 1-800-843-5678.

You should also gather pertinent information regarding your child and the person you believe has taken the child, when the disappearance occurred and where they may be heading. Photos of the child and biographic information about the child and the person they are with, other possible friends or relatives that might know where the abductor and child are going, and any specifics you may know about travel itineraries, departure routes or airlines/border crossings likely to be used would all be helpful to officials involved in the search.

If a custody order has been issued, particularly if the order grants you sole custody, restricts visitation times or prohibits your child's removal from the state, keep copies of the order and make them available to officials working to help you locate your child. Your attorney may also be able to assist in working with local law enforcement or the courts. If you have a court order that prohibits removing the child from the U.S. and a law enforcement contact, call 1-888-407-4747, or e-mail us at PreventAbduction1@state. gov. The Office of Children's Issues may be able to assist in preventing your child from departing the U.S.

In order to pursue the return of your child from another country, you may need to retain an attorney in the country where your child is located. Having an attorney abroad can help you navigate the foreign country's legal system.

For information about hiring an attorney abroad, see our section on Retaining a Foreign Attorney. Although we cannot recommend an attorney to you, most U.S. Embassies have lists of attorneys available online. Please visit the local U.S. Embassy or Consulate website for a full listing.

My Child has been abducted, but is not going internationally. What can I do?

If you believe your child has already been taken out of state, you should notify the nearest FBI field office. Be advised that some law enforcement agencies may be less responsive if there is no court order. If you have difficulty getting local law enforcement to focus on the search for your child, contact the National Center for Missing and Exploited Children's 24-hour hotline at 800-843-5678.

You should also gather pertinent information regarding your child and the person you believe has taken the child, when the disappearance occurred and where they may be heading. Photos of the child and biographic information about the child and the person they are with, other possible friends or relatives that might know where the abductor and child are going, and any specifics you may know about travel itineraries, departure routes or airlines/border crossings likely to be used would be helpful to officials involved in the search.

Where can I go for legal advice?

In order to stop your child from leaving the United States, you will likely need to retain an attorney in the state to which your child resides. Although we cannot recommend an attorney to you, an attorney in the U.S. can help you navigate the legal system and any inherent legal challenges or hurdles you face.

What federal laws exist to help prevent child abduction?

Under the laws of the United States and many foreign countries, international parental child abduction is a crime. Removing a child from the United States against another parent's wishes can be considered a crime in every U.S. state. In some cases, an abducting parent may be charged with a Federal crime under the International Parental Kidnapping Crime Act (IPKCA). Additional federal laws are also in place to assist law enforcement in preventing abductions. Be aware, that federal statutes are not the same as state statutes. Each state has its own laws and governance, and some may have provisions to stop abductions, others may be used in cases of custodial interference.

I fear that my spouse's parent's family will take the children. Can you help?

The United States does not have exit controls, so you should ask the advice of a qualified attorney who can help you to get sole custody of your child. If there is any possibility that your spouse or your spouse's family will abduct your child, you may want to get a custody order that prohibits the removal of your child from the United States by your spouse or anyone acting on his/her behalf. Without a specifically worded custody order with minor child travel restrictions, law enforcement and airline personnel may not act to prevent your child from being taken out of the United States.

If your child has a valid passport and the other parent or his/her family has it, you could ask the court to hold your child's passport.

I don't have a custody order and my spouse and I are currently going through custody proceedings. How can I prevent my child from being abducted?

You should ask the advice of a qualified attorney who can assist you to get sole custody of your child. You may want to avoid joint custody orders in families with citizenship in more than one country. If a joint custody is granted by the court, you may want to ask the court if your child can live with you most of the time.

Specify in the custody order the exact times and locations for visitation. You may want to ask the courts in the United States to only grant supervised visitation to the other parent. If there is any possibility that the other parent will abduct your child, you may want to get a custody order that prohibits the removal of the child from the United States. If your child has a valid passport and the other parent has it, you may want to ask the court to hold your child's passport. Without a specifically worded custody order with minor child travel restrictions, law enforcement and airline personnel may not act to prevent your child from being taken out of the United States.

I have a custody order that does not have travel restrictions, how can I keep my spouse from leaving the country with my child?

If you feel your spouse will abduct your child, and your current custody order does not have any travel restrictions for your child, you should ask your attorney if it is possible to add a provision to your current custody order that prohibits the removal of your child from the United States. If your child has a valid passport and the other parent has it, you can ask the court to hold your child's passport because the United States does not have exit controls. Without a specifically worded custody order with minor child travel restrictions, law enforcement and airline personnel may not act to prevent your child from being taken out of the United States.

My spouse is in the military and I don't want my child to go overseas. Can you help?

You should seek the advice of an attorney and contact the Department of Defense (DoD).

How effective are abduction prevention measures?

Prevention measures can be very effective if appropriate steps are taken in a timely manner. This includes engaging law enforcement and legal representation to advocate on your behalf and secure court documents that protect you and your child. The Children's Passport Issuance Alert Program (CPIAP) can also help to prevent a possible abduction.

What is the CPIAP program?

The Children's Passport Issuance Alert Program (CPIAP) is one of the Department's most important tools for preventing international child abduction. If a passport application is submitted for a child who is registered in the CPIAP, the program allows the Department of State, Office of Children's Issues to contact the parent(s) or legal guardian(s) who registered the child and inform them of the application.

CHAPTER 1

• • •

MATI WOVE HIS BODY TOGETHER with mine. His delicate, five-year-old frame had been pushed far beyond the point of exhaustion. As father and son, we had that in common. Now he was asleep, and although restless, this was what I had hoped would come for him, a few precious moments of peace. I had waited so long to hold my boy, though now that I had him in my arms, I couldn't let him go, not even to sleep or relieve the mounting tension in my limbs. As he shifted, finding his comfort in an ocean of chaos, I held him even tighter.

We had been hidden away in the police station for so many hours that I had lost count. People walked past us through the lobby doors into the wee morning hours. Faces gathered at the barred windows peered curiously inside. We listened to an assortment of petty criminals plead their cases while keeping one eye on the strange white man clutching his son.

Surely they must have wondered, what are they doing here?

The creeping stench from mold and layers of ancient filth had become almost unbearable. I took in shallow breaths. I covered my nose and mouth with my sweat-drenched shirt collar when I needed to draw a deeper breath. As I clutched Mati closer, I absorbed what I could from my surroundings, knowing that someday, when this ordeal was finally over, I might want to remember these details. One day, I shuddered to think, Mati might ask me to tell him some of what I remembered from our experience. I would describe the fluorescent light spilling its ugly halo from a fixture directly over our heads, how I could hear its incessant hum. The mint green paint peeled from the cracked walls, revealing the black, damp cement underneath. The corners not consumed by shadow were thick with dirt and cobwebs. We sat on the only chair we could find because the floor was filthy with wood splinters, crumbled concrete, and shards of broken glass. When I shuffled my weight on the small chair we shared, the sound of grit beneath my shoes filled the room.

Mati and I had arrived here amid the daytime hustle of police activity. Officers and uniformed soldiers came and went as we were quickly ushered down to the back room, into a small space that felt, at first glance, like the kind of place where well-guarded secrets were extracted from both guilty and innocent by harsh coercion. This was the sort of room that only existed in the movies. I had to steel my focus, putting aside the grim association. I had to remain positive, hopeful that this awful place would serve as a bridge on our road to salvation rather than a roadblock. Hours passed, and that hope endured through uncertainty.

The stifling afternoon heat and humidity had dissipated, leaving us in much more comfortable air. The daylight that had passed through the half-closed blinds was gone, replaced by inky darkness. Night had fallen, and the hustle of the police station gradually quieted, replaced by the creaks and yawns of a near empty building. Every few moments, the sound of air circulating through the ancient ductwork rattled over my head. Somewhere in a room nearby, water dripped in a staggered pattern. If my thoughts drifted far enough, I would startle as another car sped down the alley outside the window, reminding me of the threat beyond our bond.

Why are there so many cars? Does anyone sleep in this town?

I heard Mati's gentle breath rise, and I drew him closer, hoping he would remain at ease.

"What was that?" he asked drowsily. His eyes lolled far enough open so I could barely make out their almond color. He was a greasy mess, strands of his brown hair clinging to his forehead.

"A car," I said as I watched him comprehend the answer, followed by the all too familiar flash of uncertainty. "Just a car; nobody important."

I continued listening for the sound of footsteps announcing someone's arrival at the police station. Although Rafeek hadn't promised me a time, I felt increased anxiety over how long he was taking to return with news of our situation.

"Is everything OK?" Mati asked. His thin voice had been taxed by the shrieks and cries of our tumultuous day.

"No reason to worry, buddy," I said, reassuring him. I ran my hand up and down his sweat-covered back.

"Are we going back home to Florida, Daddy?"

"I'm trying, buddy," I said. "Just hold on tight, OK? We'll get out of here soon."

"Are we in danger?" he asked.

I put my hand on his bony shoulder. It took all the self-control I could muster to keep myself from shaking.

"Go back to sleep," I said. "Let me worry about that."

I'd been in contact throughout the day with the outside world via text. My contacts brought us food and water, but in the last hour, that lifeline had gone silent.

Another car sped through the alley. I held my breath, hopeful this would be the sound that led to my friend's return. I had only known him a few days, but everything rode on him.

Damn it, Rafeek. Hurry up.

Dhaka is one of the largest cities in the world. We don't often think of it as being that large and cosmopolitan, yet the sprawl from Bangladesh's capital city brings the population of the greater area to almost seventeen million people. The metropolis is roughly the same size as Baghdad; the population of the city proper is more than twice that of Berlin, Germany, and more than three times that of Houston, Texas. Hardly anyone speaks more than the few words of English necessary to beg or extract money from an American.

The size of Dhaka makes for quite a spectacle, awe-inspiring even after many years traveling there. During daylight hours, the noise outside rises to a near deafening pitch: car horns honk, people shout at one another over crowded streets, the cacophony of industry and construction, either building up or tearing down a city in a perpetual state of growth and flux.

Even the rain in Dhaka arrives with an air of violence. Every spring the torrential downpours flood the countryside and the city, drowning out everything else but their clamor.

Here we were in the heart of that Dhaka, an American citizen with my son who was an unfortunate child of two nations, whose custody hung in the balance of who next passed through that door. At this juncture, my Bangladeshi fiancée and I were embroiled in what amounted to a world war for the right to raise this boy. Burrowed down in that police station backroom, the eerie silence of exhaustion held sway over both of us. Yet somehow, I could not settle down. I could not breathe for uncertainty and revulsion. I could barely move a muscle for fear of jostling his tranquil state and having to start all of this over.

I could not focus a thought, at least not until Rafeek burst back into the room. In my fog, I had not heard his car arrive, nor his feet outside the doorway.

Somehow I had fallen asleep because I startled at his voice and the sight of his face.

"Tyler, Tyler," he said. I eased at the familiar sound of his voice. "It's just me, it's Rafeek, don't worry."

The door to our room laid wide open for the first time in what seemed like hours. I wondered without speaking, was this that door to freedom? Or would it lead to my losing Mati forever?

"Is it time to go?" I asked.

Rafeek shook his head no, but his expression remained tinged with optimism.

"It isn't?"

"No, not yet, not yet," he said. Rafeek appeared jittery, which made it difficult to determine what was happening outside. My new Bangladeshi friend was always a little tense. Now, though, he was a little more jittery than usual.

"Why can't we go now?" I asked. "It's night and the city is quiet."

Rafeek shook his head more vehemently as he crept toward the daylight window where he cocked his head and listened for a moment. When he returned to our chair, he cradled Mati's slackened head as gently as though he were his own son.

"We cannot move from here yet, Tyler," he whispered.

"I don't understand."

"Trust me, we cannot move."

"I want to get out of here now."

"Please listen," Rafeek said, eyes darting to the window.

"I am tired of listening," I replied. "I thought we were going to get out of here."

"We are."

"Well, damn it, why not now?"

"Because right now, this station is surrounded."

I shook my head and felt a lump form in my throat. I clutched the limp boy closer to my body. I thought, as I had so many times throughout that night, I wanted Mati to feel my heartbeat.

"We're surrounded?" I whispered.

"Yes, yes. Surrounded by hit men," Rafeek replied. The way he said those two words, I thought he might actually be excited. "They're hired guns sent for you, sent by her family."

"How many?" I asked.

Rafeek shrugged. "Twenty. Maybe even more than that."

"What do we do now?" I asked, now unable to restrain my terror. All those cars we had heard come and go throughout the night suddenly had a different meaning.

Rafeek smiled. He was my rock. Even though we were surrounded, his control over the moment never swayed.

"We remain calm, right my friend?" he said.

"Calm?"

"Yes, calm. Right now, there is nothing to be gained by panic."

I shifted. I heard Mati yawn, the kind of delicate sounds he would make while dreaming in the crib when he was a tiny baby, in the years before the running, before the terror and the uncertainty. The way he did before all of this.

"OK," I said. "But when do we actually get to walk out of here?"

Rafeek fixed his shirt and coat. He calmly ran a hand over his three-day stubble as he thought through the delicate steps to follow. "We go first thing in the morning."

"The morning?" I said.

"After first light, yes."

"We'll be out there in plain sight, though."

"Yes, I suppose we will," Rafeek said. "But your enemies are much less likely to take a shot if they think someone can identify them."

I closed my eyes. As I tried to absorb this grim, uncertain reality, I felt Mati's head lift slowly off my shoulder and turn toward our mutual friend.

Mati smiled. Rafeek smiled back.

Outside, lights flashed as another car raced past our line of sight. I tensed, turning just in time to catch a glimpse of the rear tire as it rolled over the broken asphalt.

"Was that . . . ?"

"Get some sleep, Tyler," Rafeek continued. "Tomorrow, believe me, you will need every bit of your strength."

I nodded, feeling myself let go. I was drowsy.

"OK," I said.

I had only known Rafeek a short while. The man that had introduced him to me, I had met only a few times. Now our lives rested firmly in their hands.

"You too, Mati," he said. "Get some rest."

Mati nodded. His head fell to my shoulder.

We would move in the morning. There was nothing else to do in that moment, so I allowed my eyes to close.

CHAPTER 2

• • •

I WAS BORN IN BOSTON, Massachusetts. I was raised near a place called Mirror Lake, a small rural community in central New Hampshire. There wasn't much there besides rugged mountains, forests, and a few sparkling rivers. The town hardly exists at all, except as a dot and name on the most detailed state maps.

Our home was hemmed in on all sides by national forest. In our yard, we had a pair of tennis courts where my father taught private lessons in the off hours after work. He was a masterful athlete. Around the time of my birth, both of my parents were working in the ski industry, and living in upstate New Hampshire proved to be an ideal location for that business. Our community sat at an idyllic crossroads for weekenders escaping from the urban bustle of Boston and New York. For many months of the year we were surrounded by white snow and winter recreation options. Those early days on Mirror Lake might be some of my furthest memories, but they are certainly some of my fondest.

When I was four years old, my parents picked up and moved. Perhaps raising a child in the isolated mountain setting spurred the transition, but we ended up moving south to the town of Newburyport, Massachusetts. When you close your eyes and picture the splendid scenes of old pictur-esque New England, colonial architecture preserved for centuries, ship captains' homes dating back to the Revolutionary War, Newburyport is the quintessence of what likely comes to mind. The entire town feels like it was plucked out of a postcard. At the delta of the Merrimack River, leading out to the seemingly endless beaches of Plum Island, the small tourist town of roughly seventeen thousand year-round residents is a perfect place to grow up.

We were an upper-middle-class family. The way I see it now, looking back, we were a hardworking, upwardly mobile family. My parents worked hard to earn everything we had. They were both professionals. By the time we moved, they were out of the ski industry. My mother took a job working in the booming local real estate business. My father managed our properties and, at heart, was an entrepreneur.

As a result of that determination, my family was well off. By that, I mean they were in a position to offer my childlike imagination a wide array of opportunity. No doors ever closed on whatever I chose to pursue. When I think back on the privilege that defined my upbringing, it involves so much more than money.

What strikes me most and resonates deepest about my childhood is that we always did everything together. We ate dinners together. We played. We went out to the movie theater. On holidays, we gathered as an extended family and celebrated as one.

On summer nights at sunset, we used to walk our golden retriever, Samantha, up and down the shores of Plum Island. In the wintertime, we returned north to ski and enjoy the pristine snow. Like any other family, we had our issues, but we were always tight. We shared common interests, a core that we could return to whenever we went astray.

My parents took a close interest in my many pursuits. They lavished time and attention on whatever I wanted to do. We were an active family, and as a result of that, my interests growing up were mostly physical. On Monday, Wednesday, and Friday afternoons after getting out of school, my father would take me down to the YMCA, the beautiful red brick rising off Market Street in downtown Newburyport.

On those afternoons, my father and I were side by side, training together in the gym. My father did not just find himself in the ski industry as purely a business venture. Life on the slopes was one of his passions. In his youth, my father had trained to become an elite gymnast and track and field star. He remained active in sports through college, and as he grew older, in his twenties and thirties, took up high-level skiing and tennis. When he was in his forties, he would turn his attention to windsurfing, a sport where he would become a professional.

On those training days we chose from a myriad of sports: swimming, diving, gymnastics, basketball, ping-pong, volleyball, and as I grew older, I took up windsurfing as well. I can still hear my father shouting encouragement, following along beside me as I trained, all the time urging me on to better my performance. We had a ping-pong table in our house. Whenever we could find a spare moment, we competed with one another. Somehow, my father managed to convey all of his tennis court wisdom to our heated matches on that table.

One of my favorite sports was diving. Even when I was a young boy, I remember working with the one-meter board, relishing quick vaults, working into a series of spins and flips. On Tuesday and Thursday afternoons, my father took me across town to the YWCA, which had an Olympic-sized swimming pool open to the public.

Unlike many of my friend's fathers who were typical men of the age, stoic or perhaps wry, offering few words of advice, mine was quite expressive. He had absolutely no fear of telling someone how he felt, especially not a member of his own family. Everyone knew they could count on him for honesty. Even though I knew my father chose his words carefully, he was an open communicator, never one to be afraid of saying exactly what he saw.

When I think back on my early diving experience, one particular afternoon after school comes to mind. My father pulled me aside as I climbed, dripping wet out of the swimming pool. Even a young boy knows when his father says one thing as a way of arriving at another truth. In that moment, I could see him wrestling with how to tell me what he really saw.

Close your eyes.

Visualize the outcomes.

Pay attention to your intentions.

If you are able to do those things, you can accomplish anything.

I began skateboarding around the age of four. I took to the sport quickly. As soon as I could find the right balance, I began to invent tricks and maneuvers.

I was always looking to push my skills further while on the board. As they did with everything else, my parents encouraged my emerging interest. On warm days, I would stay out on the streets late, until dinner time, soaring down the block, whirling around the driveway, running inside to show my parents whenever I found a new spin on a familiar move.

Skateboarding wasn't just another way to pass the time for me. As my interest in the sport blossomed and evolved, it became my springboard into the world of business.

By the early 1980s, skateboarding had become a national phenomenon. Riders were viewed as iconoclastic rule breakers. Hopping on a board and cruising the streets was what the cool kids did, and I emerged as a leader in my community. Around the fifth and sixth grades, I started selling custom-designed skateboards to the other kids in my class. I sold stickers and posters, the kind of things boys loved to plaster on their walls and notebooks.

I went away to nearby boarding school at an early age. I attended Cardigan Mountain School and Holderness, both prominent prep schools back in New Hampshire. I ended up choosing to attend college in Newport, Rhode Island, at Salve Regina University, a prestigious private Catholic institution. School came naturally to me, and I completed my education, earning a degree in business and marketing.

I began my career out of college running a real estate business on Martha's Vineyard. In my spare time, I worked a few hours as a massage therapist at a five-star spa. I continued my education, learning about the history of world monetary systems, gold, silver, and energy trading, an interest that four years later led me to a career in the hedge fund and alternative investment industry.

This was early on in the 2000s, and the business was absolutely booming. On the teetering shoulders of a swelling housing bubble, everyone seemed to have a little money to invest. These were the good days—before the bubble burst, leading to a devastating economic downturn later in the decade. After the downturn, the entire financial management industry was unfairly demonized in the media, determined to create a villain. For my part, I hooked on with a prestigious international hedge fund and set out on my career. The concept of creating and managing money was in my blood, and the financial industry was a natural fit.

From the outside, hedge funds are a curious fiscal animal. For the layperson, they're not the easiest concept to understand. Managing hedge funds requires, among other things, a keen eye for the often-slim margins between managing risk and control. I worked closely with traders, guys who fought it out on the floors all day. From them, I learned risk management. Finding that balance and knowing how to ride it as long as possible is the difference between millions and nothing at all. For me, it was like riding a rail on a skateboard. I discovered an instinct for how to hold on.

Money was never an abstract idea for me. Difficult concepts came naturally. Perhaps I was gifted. My parents possessed an entrepreneurial spirit, a trait they had passed on to me. They had taught me lessons managing the family's real estate holdings back in Newburyport.

Perhaps as a result of my parents' influence, I could see clearly what portfolios would end up profitable for my clients and which ones offered too much in the way of volatility. Good investors possess a keen sense for the difference, and I had that. My career advanced rather quickly, and I ended up spending a great deal of my post-graduate twenties working from home.

Eventually, though, I moved south to Florida. However idyllic, New England winters can take their toll. My parents were getting older and had decided to move south to a warmer climate. Being close to them remained a priority for me, and my employment through a New York firm allowed me the ideal flexibility to set up a base wherever I felt most comfortable. My parents ultimately settled in Naples, Florida, a small community on the south, gulf side of the state, and when I was twenty-nine, I picked up and moved with them.

Naples is a gorgeous city. I have traveled the globe, and it remains one of the most beautiful places I have ever seen. With a climate that remains warm all year round, it attracts a steady stream of tourists from all over the world. The streets and many parks are lined with luscious, tropical flora that is almost too beautiful to believe. On the eastern edge, the city is hemmed in by Everglades National Park, and on the western side by the warm waters of the Gulf of Mexico. North and south end in long, white sand highways.

My parents and I found side-by-side condominiums. Like before, we had found an ideal setting in which to set up our new lives.

I was just getting out of a long-term relationship when I first met Mati's mother. I wasn't necessarily seeking the woman who would eventually become the mother of my child, but that was who I found.

I was into my early thirties. My career was well established. I was thriving, in spite of the global economic downturn. Naples, Florida, was my home. My relationship with my family had never been stronger, yet I couldn't help but feel that something was missing.

The next step was something I would consider bold, at least for me. Meeting new people was always relatively easy for me. I'd never had trouble talking to strangers, striking up a conversation at a bar, in an airport, or at a party. On this matter, though, I felt some pressure to look elsewhere. All the signs told me it was time to broaden my search, to perhaps open myself up for something new.

I had never been one for going on dating websites or blind dates. My friends and colleagues would offer to set me up from time to time. I always politely refused. The situations seemed like a stretch. I wasn't desperate. Taking that number felt like a desperate measure.

Something compelled me to say yes this time. When a good friend offered an introduction to someone she knew, I was hesitant. She was persistent, though, saying that she had someone who would fit me like a glove, a woman described as exotic and sexy. I was hard pressed to refuse. Insanity is doing things the same way while expecting different results.

So, I said yes and took her number.

I was driving back home to Naples from a work meeting in Palm Beach, Florida. The drive was roughly two hours across the state, one I had made many times before. During recent days, I had connected a few times with Khadijah via telephone. She sent me pictures of herself via text message. They were stunning. I was intrigued, to say the least, so we expressed mutual interest in meeting up. Her voice was sensuous. The echo clung to my senses as I sped down the highway toward our meet up. On my way home, I would pass through Boca Raton, where Khadijah had an apartment. We decided to meet up for dinner at Truluck's, a world-renowned steak and seafood house.

My first date with Khadijah was among the most unforgettable experiences of my life. Many years later, I can attest to that fact for quite a number of reasons. Even though the nightmare of our engagement still haunts my family to this day, I can think back on those first few moments together and recognize the rare electricity that pulsed between us.

When I first laid eyes on Khadijah, she absolutely stole my breath away. The pictures she sent could hardly do her beauty justice. As we took our seats, I realized she had a similar effect on everyone she encountered. Heads turned as she passed. Men were helpless. I had been with a few beautiful women before, but Khadijah was far more exotic than I was used to dating. Something about this woman, from the first look, was intoxicating. We got cocktails and shared in small talk. Eventually our meals arrived and her seductive glances began to get the better of me. I remember thinking I had to break out my A game.

Turns out, Khadijah felt the same way; she had to get on her best game, too. We managed to sustain decent conversation throughout dinner, but both of our minds had clearly moved on elsewhere. She told me a little about herself. She had a big family that ran a prominent business back in Bangladesh. She was embroiled in a long and thorny divorce that had only recently been finalized. She confessed that she viewed herself as a free spirit at heart.

Khadijah told me she was a Muslim. She had broken away from the clutches of her parents back in Bangladesh. She was here in the United

States, seeking greater opportunity and a chance to live her life on her own terms. All throughout her upbringing, with her desire for personal freedom, she had become the black sheep in her traditional family. If she stayed, she would only fall further under their thumb. She was tired of living in this kind of shadow, so here she was.

I was due back home in Naples the next day. I never finished the trip back, though. Dinner had become a prelude to something much more intriguing.

Khadijah and I spent an uninterrupted twenty-four hours together, a night and day of almost seamless erotic exploration. We hardly came up for air.

We made a fast connection. Touching her thrilled me. Being beside her, feeling her breath, I felt refreshed. For the first time in a long time, I felt the part of something exciting. The romance that sprawled out from that first date was an absolute whirlwind. Khadijah came across to me as an open person. At first glance, she appeared to have no secrets.

She talked quite fondly about her sexuality. Khadijah was provocative and had no shame about that fact. In whatever town she was in, she was fond of frequenting high-end strip clubs and sex shops. She was a VIP in what she described as "bliss parties," underground clubs for the super wealthy and bisexual women. The way she talked about this salacious aspect of her life, one would think she was proud of her promiscuity.

Our pattern began to form. Khadijah lived ninety minutes north of Miami in the small community of Delray Beach. I would drive across the Everglades to the ocean side on Friday afternoons after work to visit her, those two nights often bleeding over into the following week. I easily performed my work from remote locations. With my laptop and phone at hand, I could stay with her as long as I wanted. Nothing held us back. I could be anywhere in the world, and in those precious moments, I chose to be with her.

Khadijah wasn't only promiscuous; she was fond of exploring the limits of her sexuality. When she invited me for a night out on the town in

Miami, I was, at first hesitant. I had not been to many strip clubs before, and was never invited in with the kind of access Khadijah revealed.

The music throbbed deeply as we approached. At first, all I could hear was the bass line from the sidewalk as I closed the car door behind her. As we got closer to the sound, Khadijah was thrilled. I could see it in her deepening swagger. As we moved down the line of ordinary guests, past the winking bouncer with hands woven together, I could hear details emerge: a cascade of siren calls, symphonic hooks rising above the drone. We were inside.

Khadijah led me by the hand, navigating the club with a keen sense of belonging. This place was one where she required no introduction, only a smile, a suggestive touch of the bouncer as they passed in the narrow hallway.

We took our place in a VIP room, within arm's reach of the DJ booth. We had some privacy, but not much. Anyone looking to the front of the stage could see anything we did.

We ordered drinks. From where we sat on the plush black leather couch, I could see the club was jumping, packed wall to wall with South Beach clientele: hot, scantily clad girls grinding against men and other women.

"Are you nervous?" she asked, eyeing the scene below.

"No," I replied confidently.

Khadijah kissed me long and passionate, eyes closed, enchanted by the music.

We touched one another, getting further into the mood. We were being fed by the DJ's intoxicating groove when I noticed another woman on the other side of our private booth. She was as gorgeous as any woman I had ever seen, her glistening skin coffee dark, her body lithe and toned. She wore nothing more than a short grass skirt and a coconut shell bikini tight over her perfectly supple breasts.

Then she smiled at Khadijah, a knowing look that drifted hypnotically over to me.

"Do you like her?" Khadijah asked.

I nodded emphatically.

"Good," the woman said as she slithered toward the couch. She wedged her tantalizingly slender body seductively between us.

As Khadijah and this stranger greeted one another, I could tell they were acquainted. They whispered. They laughed.

"Let's show Tyler how we do our thing then," the woman said.

Khadijah smiled in agreement. Her friend ground her hips against my crotch and kissed me. When I hesitated even slightly, she encouraged me to go deeper, forcing her tongue down my throat. I touched her bare flesh, felt Khadijah grind against her, hand between her thighs.

Her mouth lowered to my chest, down into my lap. My head fell back. I was blinded by the pulsing stage light. The black woman turned around and ground her pelvis against mine. Then Khadijah wedged between us, kissing us one after another, each more passionate than the last.

The music tempo picked up. My hands groped and caressed. Our bodies tangled seamlessly into a series of positions, sharing in one another, and I lost track of my surroundings.

Suddenly, I was unaware of the crowd dancing all around me.

It was the small hours of the morning when we finally left. The bouncer was gone. The line of waiting guests and red velvet rope that held them back had already rolled up inside.

Visiting a bliss party with Khadijah wasn't just a matter of drinking champagne and watching her make out with other women, though. Soon after my first time, she begged me to participate, urging me to share her with complete strangers, to try new things together. We were falling in love; at least I believed that I was, less and less able to resist her charms. Whatever our obvious cultural and religious differences might have been, this was where I wanted to be.

From the first moment we locked eyes in the lobby at Truluck's, I was monogamous. Khadijah was someone I wanted to be with, a frame of mind I took seriously. When my friends and colleagues would ask, I told them I was unavailable for any introductions. I told my family about her. As far as I was concerned, I was dating only Khadijah.

At that time, I believed she was doing the same.

I remember when we got the news as clear as though it happened only yesterday. We had been dating less than two months. On a seemingly ordinary Monday, the end of another of our long weekends together, Khadijah was leaving the apartment to get her birth control prescription refilled. For her particular medication a test was required, so she had to make a visit to her doctor instead of just the pharmacist.

As Khadijah left the house, I thought nothing of what she was doing or where she was going. As far as I was concerned, everything was fine. I kissed her gently on the cheek and told her I'd see her when she got back home. I sat on the deck, opened up my computer, and jotted down notes on some calls I had to make. I started my workday, as I always did.

Hours passed without a text message or a call. I began to worry. Her doctor's office was only a short drive away.

When Khadijah arrived back home, her demeanor had changed from when she left. I followed the sound of her footsteps from the front door, into the kitchen where she leaned against the doorframe, arms folded tight against her chest. I had known her only a short time but grew to recognize that this was the posture she took when she had been struck by an idea.

My palms dampened with anticipation as I leaned in to get a look at her wandering eyes. "What's going on, baby?" I asked.

At first she was silent, so I asked her again.

This time Khadijah turned, glanced back at me, and said, "Tyler, I'm pregnant."

The look she gave me was one I had never seen before: the look of someone who was very frightened.

"Wait?" I said. "What did you say?"

"You heard me. I'm pregnant."

I imagine the look I gave her back was similar.

CHAPTER 3

• • •

I saw no reason to debate Khadijah. To pursue the matter further would have been futile. I wasn't going to ask if she was sure. We weren't teenagers anymore. This wasn't a case of a missed period. She had received word from a screening taken at her doctor's office. We had no home pregnancy test to quibble over crosses or varying shades of blue.

As she stood across the kitchen from me, rattled to the core, her dark eyes wide with fear, the reality of our situation could not have been any clearer. This woman, who I had barely known for two months—little more than a few good times—was going to become the mother of my child. So far, we had an intense sexual chemistry but beyond that was a mystery.

When we finally calmed our anxieties and sat down, we began to unravel when Khadijah actually got pregnant, although in hindsight that hardly seemed to matter.

We traced our unborn child's conception back to a long excursion we had taken to New York City, the weekend when we met her family for the first time. I remember it vividly. We could not keep our hands off one another. Every opportunity we had to touch and kiss, we eagerly took advantage of. Khadijah and I sat wrapped up in first class. We made out passionately for almost the entire flight north from Florida to New York.

We didn't care. We wanted one another every moment we were together.

I wanted to have children. Even when I was a teenager, I had always seen myself as having a family of my own someday. When I visualized how my experience would ideally play out, I would raise those children in close proximity to my parents, in a similar way that I myself was raised. More specifically, I could see myself becoming the father to my child that my father was to me. I would be attentive, involved in all aspects of their young lives. Nothing would be too small. I would offer them each and every possible opportunity at success.

Khadijah and I could muster that passion on command. In our short time together, though, I had not exactly been convinced that she was the kind of partner who wanted to go along for the parenting experience; at least I had not yet come to that view of her character. We possessed undeniable sexual electricity. We looked good going out on the town together, but in the days following her revelation, I had to ask, did we have the kind of partnership chemistry necessary to successfully raise a family? Two months can be a long enough time. For us, though, it was hardly enough time to gauge that level of personal commitment. Now it seemed as though we were being forced to arrive at those conclusions under significant duress of making a big decision.

When the shock of Khadijah's news eventually wore off, we sat down. We chose somewhere quiet and intimate. Dinners out or a nightclub, so much the staple of our early courtship, were entirely out of the question for this kind of conversation. We had never been serious with one another before, but we had an enormous decision to make about what had rapidly evolved into our shared future and the future of the child she was carrying. I hardly knew what she felt about anything crucial, but I was about to find out her feelings on abortion.

Those days that followed were tough. Even looking back through the lens of everything that followed for us, they were some of the toughest talks I have ever endured. Spring or summer, tropics or the cold north—that didn't matter; we found ourselves in a dark place. We talked about what having a baby meant for our lives together. We weighed the sum of the many benefits we would reap upon becoming parents. We talked about the myriad of sacrifices. We'd need to be serious. We approached the process of decision making from every angle we could possibly imagine. Everything was out on the table. It had to be that way.

When it came down to the bottom line, Khadijah did not believe she was ready to become a full-time mother. Not yet, at least. She was still young. There was so much left for her to figure out about herself and her life that having a child would only get in the way.

Although I held an opposite view, I was unable to sway her decision. What a potential mother wants for her body goes a long way in these situations, and rightfully so. We weighed each of the factors, and when we were truthful, we realized we hardly knew one another. We knew we could rely on passion to keep connected, but basing such a life-changing transition into the role of a parent on that electricity did not make clear sense.

When I reflect on those days, perhaps we could have grown from the experience. Khadijah and I shed many tears together. At times our talks escalated. Our voices raised into screams of sadness and bitter frustration. During our darkest moments, we felt as though fate had forsaken us. The child she carried seemed more like our curse rather than a gift.

On a few occasions, I had to get up and walk away. I would do deep breathing exercises and yoga. I'd find anything else I could do to occupy my time: go for a drive, for a run, or a relaxing skate down the boulevard at night, only to circle back to the table and push forward.

Those days were difficult on my parents and me. As close as we had always been, I had a difficult time telling them what Khadijah and I were working out.

"Is something bothering you, Tyler?" my mom would ask.

I'd look back into the eyes of this woman I'd never lied to and shake my head. "No, Mom. Everything is fine."

As all mothers do, mine knew better, and as she would walk away and leave me to my grief-stricken pondering, the feeling of betrayal I harbored was intense.

In the end, Khadijah and I decided that we simply were not ready to have this child. Perhaps, I mused hopefully, there would be another chance for us to choose the other fate.

If we were indeed going to eliminate our pregnancy, naturally I wanted the best for Khadijah in terms of the procedure. They had to be professional and discreet. After some searching, we decided on a well-renowned women's clinic across town that seemed to fit all of our needs.

I choked back a tear as I overheard her calling to make her appointment.

"Yes," she said. "We'd like to come in and see someone about my pregnancy."

From the moment we made our choice, my heart was broken. I had never felt anything quite as awful as that ache of something lost.

I was a zombie. My usual focus at work vanished. In the days leading up to our scheduled procedure, I felt a growing angst. I was too exhausted to exercise. Sometimes I found I was almost too tired to wake to the alarm clock. I found I was anxious about everything and was even snippy with my parents but could not tell them why. All the energy I could muster went into simply maintaining an emotional balance. The way I saw things, Khadijah needed me to be strong for her, especially considering what she was about to experience. I would be selfish to insert my own grief.

We planned to get down to the clinic on the morning of our procedure. We decided it was best to get in early and get the ordeal over with as soon as possible.

Although it was still early, the weather looked to be turning out absolutely gorgeous. The blue sky was filled with brilliant sunshine. A warm and gentle breeze drifted across the white sands from the gently lapping water. As I waited outside by the car for Khadijah to come out, listening to the sound of sea birds and laughter, I remember thinking, why is this happening? There has to be a better way. She stepped slowly out the door, cracking a half smile; it seemed this was what we were stuck with.

Neither of us had slept much the night before. We tossed and turned, ignoring the obvious. For the most part, Khadijah and I drove to the clinic in silence. She leaned her tired head against the half-open window, wind whipping her black hair. She had a faraway look that tightened into one of panic as we pulled into the clinic. Conversations about our feelings all but dried up after our decision was made. Where we were, feelings had no place. Looking at her forlorn expression, my only guess was that her heart was breaking as well.

The car stopped. I dropped the keys in my coat pocket.

"Come on," I said, offering her my best tender voice.

I guided Khadijah from the car and up the flight of stairs to the clinic. She walked gingerly, as if she was already in recovery from the operation.

We stood side by side in the waiting room. I was proud of Khadijah. She did her best in those few awkward moments to put on a strong face.

"Good morning," the receptionist said.

Khadijah smiled bravely. She allowed me to do some of the talking as she choked up. We were strong. In those moments, we were there for one another like never before or after.

Her fingers were wrapped tightly up in mine. A few times as we checked in I squeezed her hand back, assuring her I was there for her.

Don't worry, baby, I tried to communicate to Khadijah through gentle touch. *Everything is going to be OK*. I didn't know if we would make it, but I knew we would make it through this ordeal.

We made this decision together, I thought as we took our seats.

Nothing on earth can prepare you for the day you go in to execute an abortion. Whether or not it is ultimately the right thing to do, something is inherently wrong. I sometimes shudder to think of anyone who enters that arrangement without conflict.

The waiting room was as sterile as I had imagined it would be. Everything seemed to be orchestrated to convey safety and comfort. White walls and ceilings surrounded us.

"You need anything?" I whispered.

Khadijah said nothing. She shook her head no.

A large saltwater tank halfway down the hallway leading out to the bathrooms was filled with colorful fish. The bubbling sound of the filter seemed almost too loud to be real. Easily distracted, I kept looking over.

Tissue boxes sat prominently on every table. Sensing one or both of us would need its contents, I gently nudged one closer. The artwork was typical for the Florida coast: simply sandy beach scenes, bright tropical fish, and setting suns. I was hypervigilant, taking in every moment's details.

We remained in that state of extended silence. My thoughts raced to nothing as Khadijah flipped through the glossy pages of a fashion magazine. I hung expectantly on her every breath.

I pretended to look over the intake paperwork, but my gaze was so unfocused I must have read and reread the same line a dozen times before tossing it on the chair beside me.

Then from somewhere behind the receptionist desk, I heard a burst of ill-timed laughter. Something about the jovial sound broke my trance.

I tensed as Khadijah turned toward it too, watching as the receptionist rose from her seat and waddled back to address one of her coworkers. Suddenly, we were all alone.

Would the laughter cue an outburst? I wondered.

"I do not want to do this," she whispered.

I placed my hand gently on her bare knee. She was cold and shaking. She had goose flesh all up and down her slender leg.

"I know you don't, Khadijah."

"I'm serious . . ."

I cleared my throat and cut her off. I was in such a state of oblivion that I could not hear the meaning in what Khadijah was saying. I was simply reciting those words and phrases I had been preparing for over the last few weeks.

"This whole ordeal will all be over soon," I said flatly. "Then you and I can sit down and talk about what comes next for us, OK?"

The nurse appeared at the doorway leading out from the lobby. With an idle wave of her hand, she showed us into the operating room where they proceeded to undress Khadijah and administer a cocktail of pain medication. She became loopy, body going limp and soft, but all the while her eyes remained intent.

We were left alone for a brief moment as the doctors prepared, when she finally spoke.

"Tyler . . . ," she whispered.

"It's going to be OK," I said, a phrase that by this time had become rote.

"I don't want to go through with this," she continued. "I want to leave."

A chill raced across my flesh. I watched as Khadijah caressed my hand in hers while she ran the other over her still-tight belly, one of those beautiful gestures of motherhood.

I listened for returning voices from the hallway, then I did a double take. Had I heard Khadijah correctly?

"Wait . . ."

"I want to have this baby, Tyler. If you still do."

"Of course I do . . ." I sprang to my feet and lifted her off the operating table. "What about your clothes?" I asked.

"Leave them," she said. "Come on."

She put her arms around my neck and held on tight. I heard the sound of the doctors coming around the corner toward the operating room.

We fled the clinic and drove away without ever looking back.

Our drive home was much different. We laughed the whole way back to my condo where we made love into the dark warmth of the afternoon.

Khadijah and I were going to welcome a baby into the world after all.

• • •

Doubt about Khadijah crept into my mind soon after we reversed our decision. When I look back with a sober eye at the myriad events surrounding our brief courtship now, though, I realize those doubts should have started much earlier.

The weekend we traveled to New York together, we were visiting the city for little more than a romantic getaway. All of Khadijah's sisters and brother were visiting the states from Bangladesh, choosing New York, where her brother lived, for their reunion.

When word came to me through Khadijah about the trip, we decided this would be the perfect opportunity to meet them all at once. Things were happening fast. They felt good, though.

Khadijah possessed a natural flair for the dramatic. She informed each of her siblings that she would make the trip but didn't tell them she planned on bringing anyone with her. In the anticipatory days leading up to the reunion, she managed to keep my company a secret from them. She thought it would be a fun idea to add a wrinkle of surprise to their reunion. We were an exciting couple, and I liked the feeling that gave me.

When I strolled coolly into the room on Khadijah's arm, a tall white guy who looked nothing like any of them, their jaws dropped in collective shock. Her family was all Muslim, degrees of traditional beliefs varying among them. Regardless, I was a former New England schoolboy who was not what they expected for their sister. The tension was heavy as Khadijah cleared her throat.

"Everyone," she said calmly, "this is Tyler."

Eyes fixed squarely on me as I shook everyone's hand. After I had been introduced, as casual as could be, Khadijah took her place among family as if nothing were wrong at all. Provocation was all part of her master plan for the weekend. She was the black sheep, after all.

"Very nice to meet you, Tyler," one of her older sisters said.

She had been the last in line to shake my hand. Out of all Khadijah's siblings, I felt right away that she was the most receptive to me. "The feeling is likewise," I said as she ushered me over to chat with her family.

The Jersey City condo Khadijah's family gathered in was gorgeous. Outside the windows, we had a view of the Statue of Liberty and a Manhattan skyline that lit up as night fell on the city. The family carried on conversations throughout the day as though I weren't there. Unable to speak Bengali other than a few words, I could hardly contribute, so I kept an eye on Khadijah and listened intently, doing my best to absorb tone and mannerisms. Their business dealt in property and retail. From what I gathered, everyone was wrapped up in the family empire.

"And you, Tyler?" her brother asked, a halfway sincere effort to include me in their sprawling conversation. "What do you do?"

I rattled off a brief description of my business. A few nods came back, but clearly my world was of no interest to them. As her brother resumed conversation on the other end, Khadijah's older sister turned back to me with a smile.

"Tell me how the two of you met."

We smiled and blushed before we launched rapaciously into our story.

I did whatever I could to charm her siblings. I tried to endear them to me, but the uphill climb proved to be extraordinarily steep. First meetings are always a challenge. In my mind, I was into this relationship with their sister for the long haul. I wasn't simply arm candy for Khadijah, there to generate shock value. I wanted to get to know everyone there as best I could.

Their shock and hesitance did nothing to dampen our enthusiasm for one another. Her older brother was well connected and had a lot of influential friends in Manhattan. After meeting and dining with everyone, we all went out to "Fuerza Bruta," an exclusive visual arts play in the heart of the city before attending an upscale house party.

Amid the crowd noise and thunderous dance music, Khadijah and I clung to one another. We saw no one else in the room besides each other. Everything else faded away.

"I love you," I said, trying desperately to raise my voice over the music.

At the same time as I spoke, her lips moved too. I could see what she was trying to say. She felt the same way. We confessed first love simultaneously.

I pulled her into my arms as the crowd pulsed around us. There was an undeniable element of kismet to our fledgling connection.

When we were done with the party, Khadijah and I hurried back to our hotel room. Nothing could keep our bodies apart that night. Our differences didn't matter. Her family's indifference had all but been forgotten in the intense heat between us. Making a good impression with her family would be a matter I dealt with on another weekend in the city.

We made love all night long. We were tireless, an unforgettable blur. The vows we uttered hung heavily in the air as we repeated the sentiment into a tapestry of love.

"Don't let me go," she whispered.

Dawn was breaking over Manhattan. The way Khadijah felt in my arms in that moment, I could have been content to stay there forever.

That was the night our son was conceived.

• • •

Almost immediately after we decided to keep the baby, I set about the complicated task of permanently binding our disparate lives. I thought we should make full commitment and get married. I began shopping for engagement rings after work. I finally settled on an impressive diamond in a classic setting. With the ring in hand, I made my plan for how I would propose.

One of Khadijah's closest friends worked as a high-end event planner. We were in Fort Lauderdale at one of her parties about a month later. The scene was elegant. Everything felt right, so I got down and proposed to her.

Khadijah wept happily from the moment she knew what I intended to do. She bubbled over with excitement as I reached a trembling hand into my pocket and revealed the ring to her.

With tears of yes in her eyes, she said yes. A stunning evening had turned memorable.

Although we were now engaged, we still lived separate lives in cities across the state from one another. I was still settled in the condo next door to my parents in Naples. My space was modest, not big but enough of a start to make our first home.

We decided the most logical choice was for Khadijah to move in with me. With a newborn child on the way, being so close to my family would be an ideal situation, considering our lack of experience with children and the amount I was traveling for work during that period of time.

One morning, my good friend brought his truck over to her old place. I managed to convince my dad to come along and help out. Together, we spent a couple of days loading all her things up and moving her across the state to Naples.

The idea of binding our lives together came with responsibilities attached. For me those developments were positive, the very things I had sought for so long. Khadijah, though, responded to those changes in quite the opposite way.

I knew Khadijah was an uninhibited girl. Trying to tame her behavior was not in my nature, though. We had electricity and I wanted to harness that. I had always wanted to share intensity with my lover and partner. When we were close, it was hot. We could be good together.

Our dating life offered a firsthand view into Khadijah's wild appetites. She fed on an array of risqué sexual behaviors. A few friends cautioned me to stay away. A girl like that is good for one night, or maybe an exciting weekend, but anything more was too much risk. I thought we could share in that uninhibited side. My hope, though, was that parenthood and our engagement would calm her down. Our new lease on life I hoped would bring a new sense of contentment in her.

I assumed that responsibility would follow naturally. Turns out, I assumed foolishly.

Work had me regularly traveling out of state and out of the country. As Khadijah moved through the first trimester and into the second, only a few days after moving into my condo, I decided I had to schedule a weeklong trip. I had an important meeting in Houston, Texas, and some business with my colleagues back up in Vermont. These would be our first real days apart.

In the days leading up to my trip, I had received a bit of distressing information. Around the time Khadijah and I were moving her into Naples, she took a trip to Las Vegas with a few of her girlfriends. She loved to party, often taking weekends away with her friends. Although I had seen my fiancée at what seemed like her most risky, I believed I had no reason to worry.

Then, only a few days later, I got an out-of-the-blue phone call from a friend, Carlo, who happened to be in Las Vegas at a stem cell research conference at the same time as Khadijah. They had run into one another while she was living it up in Las Vegas, back to her promiscuous tricks.

"Something just isn't right," my friend said straight out.

I was shocked. "What do you mean, exactly?"

We hadn't spoken in some time. Hearing from him about Khadijah took me by surprise.

My friend somehow remained stoic, refusing to divulge any specifics of what he'd seen. "Right now I don't really want to get into it, but trust me, she's not the girl for you."

The words resonated in my head. "Something just isn't right." For some reason, though, I chose to look the other way.

Perhaps I was blinded by love. Perhaps it was the whirlwind surrounding engagement and the flood of hopes that comes when you begin to embrace parenthood. Whatever I was afflicted with, I could not see what was happening. At least, not until I traveled for that first time.

I never told Khadijah about Carlo's call. I thought it better to sit on that information.

During the week I was to be away, Khadijah told me she had planned a trip. This time she was going to the Bahamas and was going to travel with Chris, a male friend.

I did not feel threatened. I had met Chris before and took him to be a stand-up guy. I had no reason to distrust Khadijah at that moment.

Turns out that Khadijah never made it to the Bahamas that week. She did travel and it was with someone named Chris, who happened to be a man, but it was not the friend I had met.

While I was gone, Khadijah traveled across the country to Aspen, Colorado. The man who accompanied her was the one she had dated before me, who just so happened to share the same name as our mutual friend. A few months pregnant, while I was working, Khadijah and her old lover spent a week together, and during that time she never told him about her pregnancy.

She managed to tell him that she was engaged, but in order to string him along, said our relationship had irreconcilable problems. As our child tossed and turned and kicked in her stomach, Khadijah told him she was considering her option to move on.

With the door left wide open, Chris took the bait. He fell back in love with his old flame. He introduced Khadijah to his family. She was four months pregnant, but they went snowmobiling and skiing, activities I would see as highly reckless since she had never been skiing or snowmobiling before.

I found out while Khadijah was still in Aspen. She didn't even have the decency to lie. We talked on the phone and she brazenly told me what she was up to. She spared no detail.

For a few fleeting moments, I felt as though someone was pranking me. The words I mustered were few but simple. I told my fiancée that she flat out needed to be a better person.

"If any of this is going to work out, Khadijah," I said, "you're going to have to be more accountable."

Awkwardly, she agreed. As we talked each other down off the ledge, though, the shock I felt radiating through my body was insurmountable.

When I returned home from business, I was livid. Khadijah sat me down. She apologized for her behavior. As best she could, she tried to convince me of her sincerity. She apologized over and over for what she called a lack of judgment.

I was skeptical. I told her we would see how things went. The trust I lost would need to be rebuilt over a period of time.

Khadijah expected immediate forgiveness. She thought simply by saying she was sorry and repeating that point, she had been absolved of responsibility.

Red flags continued to pop up. Khadijah still had a few things left to pick up from her apartment in Boca Raton. When I went there to retrieve them for her, I found obvious signs that Chris remained firmly in the picture. In fact, he clearly had been there recently.

It was my turn to confront the problem. Khadijah never even bothered to deny the affair. When I brought up what I had found, she was brash about the fact that she was cheating on me. A sad pattern of lies and infidelity was forming.

With the abrupt collapse of trust, our once vital and exciting sex life soured. Feelings of cohesion and unity are a significant aphrodisiac for me. It turns me on, on a deep level. That feeling of trust with my partner allows me to take the chance. With that thrown suddenly out the door for us, I felt a lack of interest where once there had been passion.

Chris continued his pursuit. He wrote letters. He threatened suicide if they were apart. While Khadijah and I were trying to rebuild the trust from their trip to Aspen, he stalked her.

A couple months after their trip to Aspen, Khadijah went on a yoga retreat to Arizona. The pressure I was putting on her to toe the line stressed her out. She said she needed the break.

Much like the Bahamas, though, not much yoga happened in the desert. Khadijah had gone to Arizona to be with Chris.

The revelations became shocking. She wasn't just cheating on me. While pregnant with our son, Khadijah continued her old debauched tricks. She frequented strip clubs. She went to sex parties. She made lavish hookups with strippers in champagne rooms.

I was at a loss for what to do about her behavior. I couldn't keep my eye on her every moment. The way she acted behind my back was beyond shocking. It almost didn't seem real.

As the reality settled in, I had another sit-down talk with her, one of many that sounded similar.

"Calm down," I said.

"What am I supposed to do, Tyler?" she roared, furious at being called out.

"I don't know," I said. "Try acting like a committed woman, like a mother."

Sometimes Khadijah claimed to understand where I was coming from. When our talks were over, she would agree that it would be best to rein in her reckless behavior. Each time we reconciled, I foolishly believed her that this would be the time she would change for real.

Khadijah slowly began to show a round baby bump that took over her once sleek, sexy figure. Most mothers embrace showing their pregnancy. Although they complain about discomfort, they relish the moment and the happy recognition from passersby on the streets.

Not Khadijah, though. She did whatever she could to hide the truth. Eventually she could do nothing to hide her condition. The change humbled her some.

Throughout those last months, we were on again and off again. Our relationship was without an anchor, in spite of our seemingly obvious commitments. She wore an engagement ring, the one I'd given her. Did she wear it when she was away from me? I didn't know.

The day our son Mati was born, all the trouble settled down. At least it seemed to ease for a little while as we became parents.

His birth was one of the most glorious moments of my life experience. As any honest father will confess, the birth of a son is a course-changing moment that nothing can aptly prepare you for.

Unfortunately, my parents were unable to join Khadijah and me. My father was also in a hospital room, recovering from a quadruple bypass surgery. My mother remained by his side, tending to his needs. We stayed in touch via text and phone for as long as we could, but soon Khadijah's labor progressed and became too intense and I could no longer divide my attention.

We worked through labor and delivery together. Being in that room for those long twenty-two hours as Khadijah gave birth with an amazing doula at our side, I felt transformed.

"Come on," I would urge, her sweat-slicked hand in mine.

She would close her eyes and push, soft groan rising into a more animal tone. I would harmonize, groaning and roaring with her as she pressed on.

Khadijah and I held one another tight. Love pulsed between us. When it became necessary, we cried, for joy and pain and sometimes out of sheer exhaustion. We walked the hall, talking to Mati. I sponged down her neck and offered her water. We found a strength we never knew we had.

When I finally heard his cry, I wept. I watched as the doula motioned me away from Khadijah's side.

"Here's your boy," she whispered.

I took Mati in my arms. I remember thinking of how strangely large and well-formed his fingers were as I carried him to her.

"Hi," I said. "I'm your daddy." Nothing felt corny. "I've been waiting a long time to finally meet you."

Khadijah wept as I laid him gently across her body. "Wow, Tyler," she said, still struggling to catch her breath. "He looks just like his daddy."

Mati latched to her breast immediately. Within moments, that precious bond had formed.

As I watched Khadijah become a mother right before my eyes, I clung to hope. She was a woman transformed. Holding our son for the first time and passing him along to her, I had a feeling that the dark days were over and something new had begun.

A few sleepless nights later, we finally brought Mati home to meet his grandparents. Khadijah wept softly as they took their baby grandson and showed him around. We were a family, and the hope that filled me was unbridled.

She would fall into this new role naturally, I thought. We would. Khadijah would become a strong mother to Mati and a loving wife to me. I thought the love we had for our child would transcend and that Mati would become our focus.

Khadijah's erratic behavior had, for the time being, ebbed. Something new had arrived in its place, though, and it came on the first day I arrived home and found my son gone.

What had arrived was something much more ugly, and I was ill prepared to deal with it.

CHAPTER 4

• • •

I REMEMBER THE NIGHT WE decided what to name our child. The images remain quite clear.

Khadijah and I sat beneath the backyard lanai with my parents. The scent of gardenias hung in the warm night air after a beautiful sunset.

We decided on the name Mati Shareng Schreyer Wood, a name we felt represented a fusion of east and west, our two worlds.

Mati (pronounced with an "o" sound rather than an "a" in Bengali) meant pearl; Shareng was Khadijah's family's house name, meaning merchant. Pearl merchant. My contribution was Schreyer, an old German name that had been my mother's before taking my father's in marriage.

Khadijah and I had also decided a long time ago that Mati would have my last name. He would be a Wood, a decision that seemed natural and would be significant later on in my fight.

I took some time away from work, and together we set about nesting in my condo. We had created this beautiful boy that we could hardly believe was ours, and no matter how many times we said those words to one another, they still felt too magical to believe. Khadijah and I fussed over his every need. We spent more than a few sleepless nights answering his cries.

That period of time was golden. Our lives were filling with rare moments of intangible beauty that would be, unbeknownst to me, brief and fleeting.

Since my parents lived next door to the condo Khadijah and I shared, they were fortunate to have an opportunity to see Mati grow up every day during those first few months of his life. They fussed over him too. They put our new parent worries at ease whenever they could. We would pass him around the living room like a prize. We would take turns holding him and feeding him at night, watching him sleep peacefully after laying him down in his crib. I learned little things about both of my parents I had never known before.

Whenever someone describes to me any of the many miracles of childbirth, these are the moments from my life that I envision. I meditate on the innate ability of a newborn infant to bring an already close-knit family even closer.

Khadijah made an effort to settle her lifestyle down, at least during those first few months. As bitter as I was about her behavior, I knew she loved our boy as much as I did. Khadijah didn't just pay these profound feelings lip service. After all we had been through during the pregnancy and even before, I believed she was intent on making a fresh start. I believed that not only did she have Mati's best interests at heart, but she had grown to have mine, too.

After a few months, Khadijah's family finally had a chance to meet Mati. Everyone close was introduced to him, except her father, a man I still hadn't met.

They came to Florida and took their turn playing with their nephew. Khadijah's mother held her grandson and cried. They bonded as best they could before returning home to Texas, Louisiana, and Bangladesh.

If I had sensed alienation over our obvious differences before, I felt harmony over the new life brought into our extended family. For the first time, I saw an attempt on her family's part to bond with me, the father of their dynasty's first male grandchild and his dedicated provider.

"He looks a little like you," everyone continued to say.

Khadijah's brother held Mati up out of the crib. "Sure he does," he said, oddly relieved. "He looks like his mother, too."

Her brother seemed oddly paternal, even condescending to his sister at times. Khadijah seemed to seek his approval as she showed him around our world. Yet Mati took to his uncle, falling asleep in his arms.

Laughter filled the room, something sorely missing from our first meeting. And joy, and I got to be a part of both of those experiences. My parents were allowed to meet them. Our families appeared to be blending into one.

As her family finally left, a new seed of hope grew. I was optimistic that the rocky relationship Khadijah and I had endured would continue its evolution.

Would this newborn baby bring all of us closer together? Would he be a catalyst that would bridge the gaps between our cultures that had been, prior to this, so prevalent?

I thought so. I allowed myself to believe.

As I should have foreseen, Khadijah soon became restless with her role as mother. For my fiancée, staying at home and providing constant care to a needy baby was missing something. Maybe domestic living lacked a necessary element of danger and carnal excitement. I suppose that during those first few months growing into a father, I found it easy to turn a blind eye.

It did not take long for Khadijah to regain her sexy figure. She worked at it immediately after Mati's birth. After some debate, she decided it would be a good idea to take a job.

Without any significant work experience to fall back on outside of retail, the best work Khadijah could secure was taking a job as a cocktail waitress. She talked her way into a few night shifts serving expensive drinks at a local upscale bar and nightclub called Blue Martini.

I was invested in being the provider for my family. At the time, however, forces outside of my control had tied my hands. My business had crumbled and I found myself in a state of flux. It was late in 2009. The energy and their futures markets, once exploding with opportunities for creating wealth, had abruptly spun into a chaotic state. No one was safe from the repercussions. Many people's lives took abrupt, even violent turns.

After the roof caved in, I too was, for the time, caught on the wrong side of the ledger. I had lost my shirt as the price of oil and natural gas, markets in which I owned a significant stake, plummeted to nothing practically overnight. I ended up like a thousand other traders during that volatile time, adrift and in need of a solution. Being progressively minded, though, I didn't want to cash in my chips and wait for the market to rebound only to throw myself back in headlong into the world that had burned me before. I wanted to forge something new.

Khadijah taking a job at Blue Martini wasn't my favorite idea. For the time being, though, a job gave her an opportunity to feel like she was a contributor. She got some of her restlessness out in the process. At the same time, her income also took some of the heat off of me to find a quick solution to my own ills. I thought I could focus on what my next move would eventually become. What came next could hardly be described as a phase of focus.

Soon after Khadijah took her job at Blue Martini, our golden time as a new family turned bleak. Our descent from bliss proved to be both painful and frighteningly rapid.

Before long, Khadijah's job went from part to full time. All the patrons loved her. They loved looking at her and flirting with her.

At least a few nights each week, Khadijah would come home drunk and reeking of booze. She would drive home from Blue Martini at all hours, past caring that she was wasted beyond recognition. She took her life into her hands each time she got behind the wheel of her car—both her life and the life of whomever else happened to be in the car with her at the time.

Often she would brazenly walk in through the front door, not caring that she was hours or even days later than expected. If I questioned Khadijah regarding her whereabouts, she would hiss and scream at me. She'd threaten. She'd curse, her anger constant and absurdly pitched.

"I'll make your life hell, Tyler," she would scream, staggering down the hall. At the time, I caught myself wondering how much more she could do to fulfill that promise.

I had been around the block. I understood that bar servers and workers often had a drink to unwind after a long shift on their feet. Khadijah had progressed far beyond that point, though, and to see her come home only to pretend to play the role of mother to Mati gave me an uneasy feeling. We had been down that road before, only now there was no pregnancy on which to pin my hopes.

"Mom?" I asked one afternoon out of the blue. "Can I ask you and Dad a favor?"

"Of course," she said.

My father arrived at her side. I could tell they'd been talking.

"I need to stay here for a few nights," I said, "if you don't mind."

My parents tried hard to make some sense of what was going on, but Khadijah's transformation from mother to tramp seemed to come from out of the blue. But as New Year's 2010 came around, Mati and I were living full time at my parents' house next door. The grim reality of what was going on did not seem to affect Khadijah in any way. She was merely stopping through as a mother. She would kiss Mati on the cheek, say her good-byes on her way out the door, and then would not return; not just overnight, either.

"Becoming a mother is tough on anyone," my mother reminded me. "I know because I remember, but I don't think there is anything I can say or do to help her."

She was right. The woman I believed would discover her own way as mother had gone completely off track.

Sometimes Khadijah would be gone for a couple of days, even a whole week at a time. When she eventually drifted back to our life, she would duck responsibility for her actions. She would lie. She'd gloss over the time passed. However much she denied it, what was going on behind my back seemed quite obvious to me. My fiancée was living another life, one she was not letting anyone close to her in on.

We had been down this road before when his name was Chris. Khadijah was on the prowl at the Blue Martini. She was chasing after other men, and those long nights away were those when she had successfully landed a new lover, someone who had no idea who they were getting involved with. Perhaps for one night, they didn't even care.

I tried my best to understand, but Khadijah and I had arrived in a place that was beyond my grasp of reason. I wanted to remain diplomatic, but that had been supplanted by shock.

Our fights went from merely bitter to frightening. I asked my once fiancée flat out what kind of person she wanted to be, not only to me but to her son who was now old enough to sense our increasing friction. My parents and I could not shield him forever. What kind of example did she want to set? My questions came back without answers. All I got was silence.

Had I done enough in the early days to corral Khadijah's affections? Could I have said or done anything that would have changed our track?

By nature, I felt as though I was an understanding guy. But for the first time in my life, I had to seriously wonder whether I had allowed myself to become too understanding.

We created a roller coaster pattern. Every time Khadijah and I fought about her infidelity, she made what was, for her, an effort to rebuild my trust in her. She used the skills she had to reconcile our differences. Whenever she would go out and make a fool of me, she always came crawling back, oozing with sexuality, appealing to my animalistic attraction to her body. This was all that she had to mend our broken fences, and quite soon that lost all meaning.

After an enticing weekend spent entwined as lovers, the cycle of infidelity would return. There was no magic, no appeal. She would dress up in a slinky dress and go out to work, and sure enough, she would not come home. A man gets tired of looking at the clock in wonder.

We could hold together for few days, maybe a week, but nothing strung together enough to return to those beautiful, earlier days. Those days were gone.

● ● ●

People rarely talk about parental alienation. It's a taboo subject even in our modern, hypersensitive culture where most people seem to suffer one codified mental health ailment or another. The subtle—or sometimes painfully overt—ways in which one parent undermines another remains a hush-hush, shadow conversation somehow.

A simple Internet search of the term "parental alienation" yields few results. You'll find scattered definitions of a disorder that comes across at first glance as disparate.

However, the emotional toll on parent and child is hardly open for discussion. Perhaps this is among the last remaining stigmas attached to divorce and the natural frailty of marriage, revulsion at the very idea that even well-meaning parents will use their children as innocent pawns.

Parental alienation is loosely defined as the process and result of psychological manipulation of a child into showing unwarranted fear or hostility to a parent, or their family. Reading that definition brings me pain. It clearly defines the first stages of my life as a parent.

Those early years as Mati's father were tragically short of bliss, a bottomless hole I could sometimes feel myself struggling to get out of. I was hardly given a chance to grow and evolve as a parent.

Instead, that time stands as a murky struggle in which I fought against Khadijah and her family's gross manipulation of the truth, a fight that nearly cost me everything.

Mati was hardly one year old at the time. He was at the age where he was just starting to walk on his own and speak a few rudimentary words.

Mati had arrived on the cusp of first experiences, his tender interactions with his world. What he could not convey in words came out as smiles, funny faces, and bursts of laughter. I recognized nascent recognition of his surroundings in his eyes whenever we were together.

During the spring, I had planned on taking a business trip. I was going to travel out to the Pacific Northwest with an old friend that I knew from my time on Martha's Vineyard. He was consulting on search engine optimization and had become a guru in the burgeoning technology field. The prospect of spending a few late spring days away and the opportunity to dip my toes into his world felt like a great tonic for what had turned into a period of deep uncertainty.

Our plan came together around his series of speaking engagements. We would fly first into Seattle then drive down through Portland. After that, we would drive west onto the coastal highway 101 on our way south to San Francisco where I would eventually depart for home.

Before leaving on this trip, I carefully worked out my return with Khadijah. Although everything around us felt on shaky ground during that time, I had no reason to believe that my leaving town presented any danger whatsoever. My friend and I would be traveling until the middle of June when I arranged for a flight home. I would be in Naples in time to celebrate my first Father's Day with my family and Mati.

I could tell Khadijah was itchy. She agreed to be around with Mati to pick me up, though. Being away from him was the hardest part of going away.

Excitement built as it always does for me around the dawn of a new adventure. As we parted on that morning, I was extra cautious and decided it best to reiterate our plan.

Getting out of town and on the road proved as refreshing as I'd hoped. My friend's speaking engagements were exciting, magnetic experiences that were highly informative. SEO was a new frontier and offered an opportunity to revolutionize my evolving business. In order to survive the next crash, I would branch out instead of folding inward. For the first time in what felt like a terribly long time, I was learning something new, and that refreshed me.

As we departed from Seattle for our second engagement three hours south in Portland, I texted a few times to check in with Khadijah. I was also in regular contact with my family.

On the surface, everything was fine. The weather was warm. From what I was told, Mati had been in a happy mood while I was gone.

For my first time away from home, things seemed to be going OK.

The remainder of our drive into Northern California took us on a course through some of the most gorgeous countryside in the United States. Everything felt right. Our final engagement in San Francisco was a smashing success. We had the biggest crowd, the most rabid response to material. When the presentation was over, we celebrated.

As I boarded my plane late on Saturday night to come home, I was buzzing with anticipation. When I arrived home to Naples on a red-eye flight in time for my first Father's Day, though, things rapidly changed for the worse.

On that Sunday morning, no one was there at the airport to greet me.

I tried to reach Khadijah on her phone, hopeful it was nothing more than a mix-up. As had been the case of late, though, she didn't respond. My calls went straight through to her voice mail without ringing. Either her phone was off, dead, or I was being blocked.

As I rode back home, I texted. I announced that my plane had arrived. I told her I was en route. Again, no response. I slowly filled with worry about what could be wrong.

As I entered our condo, my heart sank. Khadijah's suitcases were gone. Shoes were strewn all over the bedroom floor, and piles of clothes were all over the bed. Mati's diaper bag was gone from the closet, along with some of his clothes. All the evidence pointed to her packing for a hasty departure.

I panicked. My lingering anxiety boiled over. I called anyone I could think of. My parents hadn't seen them in days. None of my neighbors or friends had heard from her either. Mati and Khadijah had simply vanished.

Meanwhile, I texted her. I asked where she was and where she had taken Mati. She texted back randomly, responses eerily disconnected from the urgent nature of my messages to her. When I pressed her too hard, she simply cut off all responses for hours on end.

I couldn't sit still. I drove around Naples. I knocked on the doors of her friends. I checked in at Blue Martini, but she hadn't been to work since before I left for the Northwest.

I scrambled for any out-of-town connections. I called the members of her family that I had contacts for, but they had neither seen nor heard from Khadijah in awhile.

I checked in with my old yoga teacher, an empathetic older woman in whose companionship Khadijah sometimes took refuge. By now I was on the brink of tears, unable to contain my simmering rage. When I confronted her directly about whether she was harboring Khadijah, she told me they had not seen one another; again, they had not spoken in a long time.

On Monday morning, after a sleepless night, again I reached out to her oldest sister who lived in Louisiana. I pressed her on the same questions I'd asked the others.

"Have you seen Mati and Khadijah?"

"I'm sorry, Tyler," she said. "I have not."

I had no reason to doubt her. Of anyone in Khadijah's extended family, she had always been the nicest to me, dealing straight where the others had quite often come off as evasive.

"Have you heard from her then?"

"I haven't heard from my sister in weeks," she replied with a bitter laugh.

Later that morning, as I pondered what my next move should be, Khadijah called me from out of the blue. Immediately upon answering, she was hostile.

"Where are you?"

"I brought Mati for a visit to my sister in Louisiana," she said.

I cringed and balled my fists in rage.

"When will you be home?"

"Day after tomorrow, Wednesday," she replied, curtly. "My plane arrives at two o'clock."

I hung up, knowing full well I had caught her in a lie.

What Khadijah didn't know was that, after speaking with her sister, I called the cell phone company. I was desperate and knew they could locate her cell phone. From that call, I made a terrible discovery: Khadijah had never even left Naples.

I decided to play along with her charade. The lie was secondary. By now, all I wanted was to see my son. But I had to be careful. Khadijah had gone to this absurd measure to keep him from me, and there was no telling what other vindictive behavior she might stoop to.

I went to the airport at the time she told me her plane would arrive. I was ready to pick Khadijah and Mati up, knowing how easily she could stage a false arrival back home.

As I expected, Khadijah and Mati never got off a plane.

I texted Khadijah when I got home. She had the audacity to respond that she'd had a friend pick her up from the airport and that she would be back home with Mati soon.

I held back my fury. I did the only thing I felt I could at that time. I waited.

Hours later, Khadijah burst through the door, Mati in her arms. She dropped her bags on the floor and, with a look of disdain, handed my son over to me.

"You go and take a trip," she said. "We take a trip too." Then she simply walked away.

I never let Khadijah know that I was on to her lies. I never confronted her regarding my call to the cell phone company. I didn't tell her that her sister had given her up either.

We had entered a new reality, one where I needed to play smart.

CHAPTER 5

• • •

As I LOOK AT THE definition of parental alienation, I never thought that would become my life. Yet every single day, I felt my family being cut further out of the picture. No calls. No letters.

The long-term psychological damage brought on by alienation is not a fabrication. Estrangement from family is a frequent result, even after resolution. Latent mental illness crops up often in children whose affections are used as leverage in marital disputes.

At the core, the offending parent who seeks to alienate the opposite partner ultimately alienates the child they would claim to love. Those repercussions might not show up for years.

Parental alienation isn't about the long term; it's about immediate gratification. No matter how strong a person might be at their core, prolonged alienation can erode even the most confident parent's fortitude. My intentions were right. My thoughts were always with him.

And no matter how strong my mind remained during those bleak days, the broken heart I carried around never quite mended. Even time couldn't make me immune to the pain. I began to see myself differently whenever I looked in the mirror. I felt the fester of my wounds.

The psychological toll on the child is real. The ravages for the parent on the outside looking in, though, are equally prevalent. Perhaps someone could say that I was not quite innocent; neither of us could make that claim. I had even been complicit, allowing her to ebb back so many times. I had moments of weakness, but that weakness should never have led to this.

The fact was, Khadijah and I had a very bad relationship. Maybe we deserved some scorn for what we'd gotten ourselves into, but this was too much.

Something had to change.

Like me, Khadijah's sister had been down this road with Khadijah many times before. She said, "I'm tired of covering up for all of their lies."

"What do you mean, their lies?"

This pattern wasn't new. As it turned out, my former fiancée's bad behavior hadn't started with me. She had been untrustworthy for as long as they had been sisters.

As we talked, I learned that Khadijah wasn't alone in her family exhibiting parental alienation. As her older sister confided, their mother would often do the exact same thing. On a whim, sometimes for no reason, she would flee Bangladesh for the United States. She would make claims that her husband didn't love her enough. To frighten him, she would scream threats to take the children away and never come home.

Khadijah had learned from watching. The familial pattern was laid out clearly; it had been right before my eyes the entire time. Only I chose not to see it.

It hadn't taken long after having a child before Khadijah started spreading herself around. She had been courting other men, all the while raising our child and staying in what was supposed to be our home. Our engagement didn't just break when I found out; it shattered.

As strange and as tenuous as things had been between Khadijah and I, they could very well end up getting much worse, I realized as I began strategizing. We had been in a tender place, but now we were teetering on a disaster with horrendous consequences.

I recognized that Khadijah would always be the boy's mother. The maternal relationship was one the courts had traditionally sided strongly in favor of. If I shook up the apple cart too much with her, I could lose my bond with Mati, perhaps forever. The episode on Father's Day would have looked like a picnic.

After a few days cooling off from the Father's Day debacle, I decided to move in with my parents full time. I could stay close to Mati and still do things with him throughout the summer.

This time the move away from Khadijah would be more permanent. I wouldn't pack a bag in hopes of coming home in a few days. I didn't consider us separated anymore.

We were over, and all that remained for us was to work out what mattered for our son.

Maybe, I thought, if we did not have to see one another every day and share the same tight space, some of the tensions might begin to ease; at least, I hoped, the potential for anything dramatic would decrease. We passed him back and forth. We shared information.

"What did you and Mommy do today?" I would ask, taking him up in my arms on a walk through the neighborhood or down to the beach.

Mati would chirp playfully, still oblivious to what was happening to us. We'd go down to the beach and play at his behest.

My parents were instrumental. They expressed relief that we'd never married, their opinion that I had dodged a bullet.

But had I?

What kind of woman had I fallen in with? Had Khadijah ever loved me at all? I thought back on that night in New York, the magic of it, and felt the pangs of bittersweet.

Had that love simply been another lie she told to extract another level of control?

I had decided that Khadijah and I could successfully work together as Mati's coparents, but we would never be getting back together for the child.

Almost immediately after Khadijah was rid of me on a daily basis, we found ourselves at the heart of a scandal. Our quiet, tranquil neighborhood would be rocked.

My neighbor, a woman my family and I counted among our friends, called me one morning as I was settling back into working.

"What's going on at your place?" she asked, her voice tight with concern.

"What do you mean?"

"I mean, with her," she stammered. "With Khadijah."

I gently tried to explain the arrangement Khadijah and I had made. We were living and raising Mati in separate homes, which should have seemed logical, but she pressed me further.

"Are you sure there's nothing going on, Tyler?"

When she didn't seem satisfied with my explanation, I pressed.

"I saw Khadijah," she said, finally. "She was showing a man out of your house this morning."

"A man?" I asked.

My jaw hit the floor, although in hindsight I should have hardly been surprised at all.

"More than that, Tyler," she said. "She's got to calm down."

My neighbor had seen one of Khadijah's overnight male guests come out of the condo that morning. As she went on to describe, though, on other mornings, she had seen others.

"She has no right to embarrass you," she said.

Sometimes she had seen two and three men at a time walking nonchalantly from my condo to their cars. I was sickened by the classless display.

We had just come home from a visit to Khadijah's brother in New York City. Since Mati had been born, we had seen a whole lot more of her family. There was little I could do to protest the trip. Everything was hanging together by a thread, and I was still trying to hold it in place.

We traveled together, and anyone looking would have seen us as a young family, even though we were anything but. Khadijah was playing her mind games. She expressed affections, behaving in an outwardly friendly manner one minute and the next undermining me. Her life was all a charade. She was playing a high-stakes game of chess, and I had no choice but to play along.

Khadijah's brother sought me out after we ate dinner. In our previous meetings, he had come across as collegial, decent even. He had an ulterior motive in his approach, however.

"Don't marry my sister, Tyler," he said, slapping me on my shoulder. "You're a good guy."

I was flummoxed. What could I say to his warning? Whatever words came to mind in those moments were quickly dashed as he leaned in closer.

"But if you decide to try and keep Mati from going to Bangladesh with her," he whispered, "I'll get the best lawyers money can buy and make your life a living hell. Do whatever you need to do now to let him go."

Panic set in. I felt the urge to sob uncontrollably as Khadijah coldly watched from across the table.

"I've got to use the restroom," I said and fled to privacy where I burst into tears. Somehow, moments later, I managed to compose myself and return to the table.

Her brother didn't say another word. The message had been delivered, loud and clear. The charade of pretending we were something else was over. Khadijah and I were at war.

When we returned home to Naples, she insisted that she travel to Bangladesh. Whether or not I went was an immaterial matter, but she wanted Mati there.

I resisted. We had just seen her family in New York. I didn't want to travel again. Besides, I pleaded, he's barely eighteen months old.

I did some research on my own. Legal representation on the level I needed was cost prohibitive. The only real ace I held proved significant: Mati's passport. Even though he was still at a tender age, he still needed documents to travel abroad. An American passport required both parents' signatures. I wasn't about to give those to Khadijah without some guarantee.

Our feud intensified. Day after day we bickered about the passport, until one evening around nine o'clock, Khadijah reached her boiling point.

I was sitting on the front room couch, Mati cradled in my arms. The debate about Mati's passport had escalated once again, this time into screams. Suddenly, from out of nowhere, Khadijah began hitting me. I did what I could to shield Mati, but she was swinging blind.

Finally, I managed to gain the upper hand. I let her fall frantically into the couch. I swung around and pressed my body down on hers, doing what I could to subdue her rage. She groaned and cursed at me for what seemed like forever until she finally settled down.

When I let my body off of hers, Khadijah scrambled for her phone and dialed. I could see what she was doing and ran next door to grab my parents. I was being framed. As my parents escorted me to the other side of the condo, I opened my iPhone and pressed record.

"I hate you mother fuckers," she screamed as my parents came through the door. My mother scooped up Mati. We tried consoling Khadijah, but there was no going back.

Within what seemed like seconds, officers from the Naples police arrived. Khadijah screamed and accused me of assault, showing off what she referred to as scrapes and bruises while I calmly stood back and watched her. She was making a spectacle, and from the looks on the officers' faces, I wasn't the only one who took notice.

Finally, one of the officers took me by the arm and led me outside. I think he was doing what he could to keep the peace. I agreed, leaving my iPhone recording inside on the table.

As I walked out with the officer into the sea of flashing police lights and took a deep breath, I found the entire neighborhood staring back at me. I was humiliated.

Khadijah ranted and raved as long as the officers would listen. I watched through the front window as she tried to curry sympathy, going back through the details of our altercation over and over while my parents witnessed her charade.

Finally, the officer who had been with her came outside. He had a conflicted look, one I could tell didn't bode well for me in the immediate sense.

They wanted to take me to jail for the night, simply to let things cool off. I had no choice. For the first time in my life, I spent the night in the county jail.

Khadijah and I had reached our point of no return. Simply living separately would not be enough to ensure harmony, let alone constructive coparenting.

A formal "parenting agreement" is a document that becomes a legal part of any divorce or court-arranged separation where a child's shared custody might become involved. Although Khadijah and I were thankfully never married in a legal sense, we were clearly in need of arbitration to dissolve our relationship. I had no trust in her anymore, and I needed to move on and start seeking joy and peace in my life again. Creating distance from her was a necessary part of that focus, and for that, my rights needed to be formalized.

Most parenting agreements cover basic matters, what anyone on the outside might describe as common sense: the child's custody in terms of legality and duration of time, the logistics of transportation and exchanges, even down to social activities and who gets what holiday. We would need to agree on how exchanges would be made and who initiated contact. In a perfect world, the agreement is mutually derived and outlines the responsibilities and expectations as a means of avoiding conflict later on. We had no such luck.

One of the key elements these agreements cover for people in our situation was communication around relocation and international travel. Everything gets spelled out. Nothing gets left to chance. If we both came from families in the United States, we would have never needed to go as far as we did in hashing out our agreement.

Khadijah had been married to a Jewish attorney before marrying me. Prior to that she had been a black sheep, but that relationship made her a pariah.

Her brother, always a diplomat, told me, "I don't know what to do about Khadijah, Tyler," he said. "She only comes to me when she wants money."

Khadijah had been living on favors, whatever she could extort or get on a handout from her wealthy family. That patience had run out, though. After years of taking, Khadijah's family had finally decided to cut her off financially. According to them, she was making a mockery of herself in the United States. They wanted her to come back to Bangladesh immediately, perhaps for no reason other than to keep an eye on her. Without gainful employment or the means of finding steady support, her only route to custody was to get her son back to her family in Bangladesh, a threat she made to my family often.

If our voices even threatened to rise beyond a hush, she'd make a dramatic move as though she were going to take him away.

Whenever we argued, which was increasing as we tried to hammer out an agreement, she would disappear afterward. She would run off for days on end with Mati without an explanation and without an agreement. I was helpless. Seclusion was her bread and butter means of striking fear into me that the next time she wouldn't come back.

She knew quite well that if I lost Mati, I would crumble under the grief. My family would end up devastated. There was no way I could allow her to manipulate the situation so freely.

Beyond my fear of alienation, I had no reason to try and keep Mati away from his roots. The way I envisioned our ideal arrangement, everything would be on the table for him. I wanted the world for my boy; our struggles would not change that. I saw his Bengali family as a crucial part of his heritage and saw no reason we couldn't accommodate those needs.

Whenever we talked about a resolution, I always broached the topic of working out special travel arrangements. I needed compromise.

In Khadijah's mind, custody of Mati was an all-or-nothing proposition. She may have wanted to be a part of a peace accord, but she wasn't compromising as a means of getting there.

Months passed. Our agreement hung on whether or not we could agree on how to span half the world between what would be Mati's two homes. One way or another, she was going to Bangladesh and he would be going with her.

Eventually, I had to concede to Khadijah her right to take Mati outside of the country. That limbo state had eaten away too much of my life, of our life. I could continue to fight, but I had already tried that route. Better to make peace, I thought, and hope for the best.

What we arrived at seemed quite simple: Mati would spend six months in Dhaka, Bangladesh, with Khadijah followed by six months in Naples with me. Everything was in writing and we signed off. When six months was up, I would get Mati back from Khadijah. Until then, she would leave with him.

On Mati's first trip, I escorted him. We had a heartbreaking good-bye. I did what I could to keep up my morale, but everything felt like a failure—first, a failure to stay together, and now a failure to keep Mati close.

When it was my turn to get Mati in July, Khadijah lingered past our deadline then demanded that I pay their travel fare back. Reluctantly, even though I had no legal obligation, I bought their tickets. When they got to Florida, I attempted to take them to court for a violation of our agreement, but I lost on a technicality. We were each entitled to Mati for six months in any given year, but nowhere in the agreement was it stated which six months those would be. Although Mati was back in Florida, I felt like I was losing the battle as well as the war.

Two years after returning home to Dhaka, Khadijah was married. It seemed as though the gears of arranged marriage had been moving while we were working out our agreement.

Her new husband was named Nabil. I knew this would happen. Khadijah was never good on her own. Whether it was me, her family, or any one of the hosts of strangers she would fly to every night, someone had to provide for her. Without support, she was bound to crumble. I met Nabil on the second pass off in Miami when they came to take Mati back to Bangladesh.

Regular updates and communication with Mati were also part of the agreement we had made. As we signed off, I felt as though I were making the best of an otherwise awful situation. He was nearing his fourth birthday. If Mati couldn't be with me all of the time, which was my first choice, I wanted to make damn sure I knew about his development and his whereabouts.

When my communication with them increased in intensity, they'd let Mati talk, long enough to placate my anger. His sweetness was so welcome but so painful to let go of when our time was up.

Khadijah's signature on our agreement was as worthless as her word had been all that time. As soon as she was legally allowed to take him away from me to her family in Bangladesh, our communication became radically inconsistent. When we did manage to exchange a few emails, they were hasty and fraught with antagonism. Regardless of how nicely I asked Khadijah, she refused to offer any substantial updates about our son's development. He was growing up, and I had no idea what that looked like.

The agreement we made was all but rubbish before the ink was dry. Arranging for his travel back to Naples was even more heated. Khadijah was always late in delivering Mati to me. Something always got in the way. She was far better at making excuses than meeting deadlines. I should have known she wasn't capable of changing for the better.

I got sporadic information from Khadijah's sister. I sent emails out to Khadijah, and phone calls to her brother and other members of her family, but they went nowhere.

Mati was not allowed to communicate with me as frequently as detailed in our agreement. We would set up a time to connect via Skype, usually early in the morning my time, only I would end up waiting by the computer.

When Mati was allowed to talk, though, the situation hadn't simply deteriorated; it had become downright eerie. He would refer to me as Tyler. He balked at the impulse to call me Dad. When I demanded to know why, Khadijah said that Nabil would be called "Daddy."

As Mati sat in front of the computer, hardly able to see the camera, he was uneasy. His bright eyes would be shifty and fearful. He seemed nervous about saying something wrong.

Seeing my boy nervous made me sad, yet I was helpless to do anything but my best to appear strong for him. I'd sit up close to the camera. I would say encouraging things to him. Grammy and Grampa Woody would join in on the call. No matter what we did, though, I could not look past the impression that he, too, knew something was wrong but was helpless to affect change.

One day I remember quite clearly, Mati's servant walked out of the room. Finally alone and free to speak, he became excited.

"Mommy doesn't want me to go to Florida," he said, looking up into the camera with his soft brown eyes.

"What?" I asked. "Is that what she said?" I choked back my fear, maintaining the obvious charade to keep him talking.

"No. That's OK." Mati's eyes darted nervously around the room. "If she doesn't let me go to Florida with you, you can call the cops on her."

When March of 2014 arrived, I felt increasingly desperate. Although Mati was due to come home to Florida in just three short months according to the agreement, a date I joyfully anticipated, I felt as though my chances of seeing him were slim at best.

Over that winter, Khadijah's sister had informed me that Khadijah was pregnant. She was going to have a little girl with Nabil the following summer. Her sister tried to come across as optimistic, but she couldn't help but express a familiar sense of trepidation in delivering the news.

Khadijah's pregnancy implied dire complications for me, however. Based on her due date, July would likely fall somewhere in the first few months of her new baby's life, a fact that would conveniently complicate her ability to travel overseas.

I had to get ahead of the excuses I was certain were coming my way. I posed direct questions about her state of health. I made offers to pick Mati up earlier than agreed upon. I could move nearby, somewhere like Thailand where I could make a quick flight to get him myself if she needed me to do so.

But Khadijah stonewalled me. She hardly acknowledged that she was pregnant, let alone showed a desire to compromise. Spring pressed into those first days of summer, and I was without an acceptable course of action.

Then I got the word I'd been dreading all along. Khadijah emailed. Her doctors had advised her to avoid flying. She offered to bring him at the end of the summer after their baby was old enough.

Absolutely not, I thought. There was no way I would allow that to happen.

My course of action seemed quite clear. If Khadijah was indeed refusing to bring Mati back to me, then I would go there. Nothing in our parenting agreement prevented that.

I had slowly built my business back to somewhere near premarket collapse conditions. I was able to do business anywhere in the world I could hook into a phone and Wi-Fi. I had time on my hands, and I had the means.

Soon after Khadijah delivered her blow, I planned my trip overseas. I looked at rental apartments in Thailand and in Bangladesh. In advance of my departure, I called on the US State Department and the FBI to let them know of my situation as an American citizen, but there was nothing they could do. Their hands were tied as long as Khadijah had me on a legal technicality.

Whether you're flying first class or coach, the flight from Florida to Bangladesh is twenty-two grueling hours. I remained focused. I read *A Father's Love* by David Goldman. I got myself into a positive frame of mind. I was going to get Mati and bring him back. Whatever nonsense document Khadijah wanted me to sign off on that absolved her of accountability, I would gladly put pen to paper on, as long as on the return flight we were together.

I was flying blind, though. I didn't know where Khadijah lived. I knew where her parents had a house and that Mati was going to the Mastermind School in Dhaka. That was the extent of my information as I got on that plane. I held negativity back. I focused my conscious thoughts on what seemed the most important. I had to do everything I could to defer my rage at her and her enabling family. This could not become about our alienation or the dissolution of my relationship with Khadijah. Anger had to come second. This was about getting my son.

I was flying halfway around the world to get what I deserved as a father. As the plane got close to Dhaka, I became more assured of that fact.

Hazrat Shahjalal International Airport is located in the north end of the city. Hardly modern, the massive terminals exist in an advanced state of disrepair, a generation behind in terms of service and amenities. The scaffolding constructing the building was built of rickety bamboo. The sky approaching the city becomes dense with smog, choking as you step out into the hot air.

The cab stands are pure havoc, the buzz of traffic and honking of horns constant. Everywhere ragged people beg aggressively for change. Drivers jack knife their way recklessly toward the curb, shouting back at one another in clipped Bengali, only to turn to their best broken English for the six-foot-four-inch American stepping out into the scorching hot sun.

"Radisson Blue," I said as I opened the back door and stepped inside.

The driver signaled and raced out into traffic toward the hotel.

The Radisson Blue is the best hotel in Dhaka. It serves luxury and business travelers from all over. Most important to me, it was the safest, offering an opportunity of a haven within the chaos.

As I arrived, I contacted my family to tell them I had arrived safely. I set up my base of operations in my room. I texted Khadijah to tell her I was in town and would be at her parents' house first thing tomorrow morning to pick him up. Then I booked a driver for the day through the hotel's concierge desk. I went to bed feeling I was as prepared as I could be.

The next day my car brought me across town to Khadijah's parents' house. I went to the door where I was greeted by servants and her mother, who seemed oddly welcoming. Everything was a game with them, so I regarded them with caution.

As I stepped inside, I looked around for Mati, but he was nowhere to be found. They said he was still at school. When I turned back to say I would go to get him, they urged me to be calm and offered to let me stay and wait for him. They said he would be home any minute.

I was respectful. My rage remained in check. I begrudgingly agreed and stood around as their house staff prepared for lunch guests, waiting for Mati to get home from school.

I'll never forget the moment when Mati came through the door and he saw me standing there. He was surprised. He was joyful, although restrained.

Most of all, though, he wasn't sure what to say. We embraced, his eyes darting anxiously back and forth across the faces of his Bangladeshi family.

He stammered, "Hey . . . Tyler."

I was crestfallen but did my best not to show it. Nabil and Khadijah smiled, so I smiled too. They wouldn't get the best of me. I had been waiting for this for many months.

As Mati and I tried to make a line for the door, we were interrupted. It was almost lunch, and no matter how hard I resisted, her family insisted that we stay and eat with them.

"It's Mati and Daddy time," I said. "We've got to go."

They persisted, though, unwilling to take no for an answer. The meal, they said, was being served in some formal manner, and it would be rude if we didn't join them at the table.

I swallowed back the urge to say anything I might regret and agreed. No matter how indignant my feeling, I had to do whatever I could to keep the peace.

The meal could not have been any more awkward. For the life of me, I can't remember what they were celebrating. The estranged, alienated father reconnected with his son in a formal dining room with Khadijah and her new baby daughter, Madison, along with her new husband, Nabil, and her mother. Rows of faceless servants waited on our every need. Not one of them flinched when Mati would cry out in joy.

Let it be awkward for them, I thought. I don't care. I had Mati in the flesh with me. He was no longer a lonesome face staring back on the computer screen or the subject of another bitter conversation. We were together again, and we were feeding off of one another.

When we were free to go, I felt like I was being released from jail after a long sentence. We jumped into the backseat of our rented car where I held him tight. For a fleeting moment, I almost forgot that we hadn't escaped yet. I didn't care.

We drove back toward the Radisson, father and son finally reunited. I didn't look back to see if we were being followed. It didn't matter. Once we crossed into the hotel, we'd be safe.

Mati and I laughed together. We joked around. There wasn't much to be shared between us that could be expressed with words. We were making up for lost playtime in giggles and expression. We took a series of selfies with my phone, so many that we couldn't count.

At a stop sign near the hotel, the car slowed to a halt. Suddenly, Mati quieted down. Something outside had seized his attention. He looked out the windows at the countless army of disheveled homeless staggering empty eyed toward the car with their hands out.

"What is it, son?"

Mati pointed quickly then pressed his little index finger to his lips. "Don't talk, Daddy," he whispered seriously. "Don't talk to the monsters."

As we drove away, I saw babies in stained rags. I saw children picking through trash heaps. We were far away from home. We were in his world, and it brought me chills.

For Mati and I, what came next was fate.

I had no idea that particular afternoon would alter the course of our journey. My life was tough at the time. Sometimes in my struggle, I lost sight of the bigger picture. When I look back on this ordeal, had anything that day gone differently, Mati wouldn't be here. I wouldn't be here.

When we got to our room, I turned the computer on and connected with my parents via Skype. They had been halfway across the world, waiting on pins and needles for any update of my next move. Though it was late at night in Florida, they could not wait till morning to see him.

I held my son up to the camera. I made him laugh. He made me laugh, too. We cried many tears of joy, more than even my mom could hide.

"That's what I'm talking about," Mati shouted. "I'm going to Florida."

It was a joyous moment. A sense of relief finally came over me. I'm sure a similar feeling came over Mati, too. He was cutting loose, I could feel it. However fleeting these moments might be, I let that feeling overcome me.

I never let on to him that we weren't out of the woods yet.

Eventually, my parents had to say their tearful good-byes. We promised to reconnect later the next day. Mati and I had the rest of the afternoon at our disposal, and I was ready to continue our good time. Without hesitation, we snatched towels off the rack and made for the door. After a long day, a dip in the hotel's massive outdoor pool sounded fantastic.

The hotel pool was peaceful. Surrounded by lush, tropical gardens, it was seemingly our oasis in a cruel and uncertain world.

During the heat of a July day in Dhaka, Mati and I jumped in the water together. The water warmed our bodies instantly as it surrounded us. We played around for a few moments, joking and splashing and outdoing one another with tricks, but before long, we drew back in close.

When we tired, we found a massive outdoor lounge bed. We laid out under the shade umbrella and shared drinks and snacks. I wasn't aware of what was going on around me. I knew I had accomplished what I set out to do, but I also knew there was so much more to come.

At the moment, though, I was trying to make up for months of lost time.

I never saw the man's face. Mati and I were too busy reconnecting. That afternoon, he was the only other person at the hotel pool where we played. Like any other businessman or tourist, he sat at his lounge chair poolside, minding his business waiting out the heat of the day.

Only this man wasn't a tourist.

He was of ordinary height and ordinary build. If I had passed the man in a shopping mall, I probably would have looked past him without a second thought. If we had crossed one another's paths in a busy airport, we would have lightly regarded one another. Perhaps we would have exchanged a few words before going our separate ways.

Yet fatefully, this man lowered his drink in order to focus his attention on Mati and me as we leapt from the lounge chairs back in the water.

He would become my ally and our friend. At the end of our ordeal, I would consider him to be a brother for life. I would soon learn that the man's name was Hans.

"Can I get you another drink, sir?"

Hans motioned yes, chasing the bartender back. "Have you ever seen that man before?" he asked, pointing across the water where I held Mati in my arms.

The bartender shrugged indifferently. "No. Why do you ask?"

"Because," Hans replied, "well, there appears to be something quite remarkable between him and that boy."

CHAPTER 6

• • •

HANS CARRIED HIMSELF WITH AN air of distinction. That was because he was, in every meaning of the word, distinct.

After watching the tender reunion that Mati and I had just experienced in the swimming pool, Hans showed no hesitation in jumping in and introducing himself to us.

"Nice to meet you," I said. "I'm Tyler."

"Hans," he said, taking my hand in his round, bearlike grip. "Likewise."

Meeting Hans felt natural. Before too long, we welcomed him to join in on the fun and conversation, and I watched as he dove in and splashed around carefree in the warm, blue pool waters.

He is like I am with the water, I thought.

Perhaps above all other things, Hans possessed a curious eye and an aptitude for keeping up an intense and intimate conversation.

Within a few moments of introducing myself to him, I could tell that Hans was no ordinary acquaintance. He was an older man, already in his late fifties. In spite of his age, Hans was sharp. Other men at that age might wind down, but not Hans. He was razor sharp in how he looked and dressed, and how he carried himself with an unmistakably charismatic air.

Hans told me that back home he had two grown boys of his own. Although both of his sons were already in their twenties and living out of the house, he was still an active, attentive father. The joy of that relationship was still alive in him. Hans had been around the world, evidenced by his exquisite tastes and appreciation for some of the finer things that really mattered.

As Hans and I got acquainted, I learned he had recently purchased a piece of real estate that was rather close to somewhere I had lived in Costa Rica.

It seemed as though months had gone by since I had last told my story to anyone, at least told it from the beginning. Yet, as we all played around in the pool together, I unloaded, telling Hans many of the relevant points of my saga. He listened with rapt interest.

Later on, as the afternoon progressed into evening, I told Hans the story about how I first met Khadijah. I told him about the disintegration of our relationship, leading up to her abduction of Mati in Bangladesh. I even managed to vent a little bit to him about how awkward our lunch had been at her family's home just a few short hours ago.

His smiles and laughs felt good. I was relieved to be getting some of that nasty weight off my chest.

All the while we talked, Hans watched Mati play. He nodded and glanced over at me as I regaled him with the intricacy of my woes, but I could see he understood what was important.

I could tell Hans instinctively knew my sadness was about the boy.

"At least you're able to be here now," he said with arms spread wide. "This is one of the best hotels in Dhaka."

I heard Mati explode with a fit of laughter as he scampered across the pool deck and flung himself into the water, followed by a great splash.

The sun fell behind the hotel. It was time for us to leave. I thanked Hans again for sharing his afternoon with Mati and me. As we said our good-byes, he gave me his phone number and offered to stay in touch.

The whole time we walked away, Hans watched us with a wide, welcome smile. Mati was exhausted. The elevator doors closed us inside and carried us up to our room.

Tomorrow morning, I thought, *is when I will start the necessary work.* All I wanted was to bring Mati home to Florida so we could have our six months together.

The courts back at home would have to decide whether or not Khadijah was in violation of the parenting agreement. What stood clearly in my way of a return trip to Florida was the matter of not having Mati's passport in hand. He needed valid documentation to travel out of Bangladesh, and Khadijah, clinging desperately to any means of controlling us, was holding his American passport hostage.

Conversation with Khadijah around that time was at best tense; most of the time her demeanor was hostile or standoffish. She was cruel, critical of me and my family. She wouldn't listen to reason. All she could do was fight and scheme.

Khadijah finally told me what she wanted. She wanted me to sign off on an affidavit, a written document that absolved her of any violation of the parenting agreement we had in place back in the states. As I mulled over her request, I could see it was nothing more than a charade. Without giving it much more thought, I told her to get whatever papers she wanted together and I'd sign them, as long as I got Mati's passport and we were able to return back home again. After that conversation, we tentatively agreed to meet up and take care of this signing within the next couple of days, long enough for her to have someone draft the paperwork.

We spent a great deal of time with Hans throughout the following afternoon. As Mati romped and played, we got to know one another quite well. It felt strange that we had only known each other a short time. We talked a lot about his business, and I talked about my career in finance. Talking about something relatively stress free felt good.

Mati adored Hans, and the feeling was mutual. I could see that my son handled himself quite admirably with adults. I was proud of how he got along with Hans.

The night after we first met, Hans, Mati, and I made plans to have dinner at the penthouse restaurant in the hotel. As we dined and drank and talked that evening, I felt a strong bond of friendship growing between Hans and me. Our senses of humor meshed well. We spoke a similar language.

Most importantly, though, during this time of stress and uncertain solitude, I developed a belief that I could somehow trust the man.

Meanwhile, Khadijah was never short on surprises.

We had tentatively arranged for her to come meet us at the hotel. She and Nabil would bring some of Mati's things, along with their documents. The plan seemed simple enough.

Khadijah and Nabil arrived, but they carried no luggage with them. They had brought none of Mati's clothes or things for the trip home. They came empty-handed, with not even the affidavit that Khadijah wanted me to sign off on to somehow absolve her of her reckless behavior. Only my son's presence kept my fury in check.

"What is the meaning of this?" I asked as I rose out of my lounge chair. "I thought we had an agreement on what this would be."

"We'll go back to the house," Khadijah said. "We'll gather his things and Mati can also say a proper good-bye to his family."

I could tell by her look that she was furious to make even this concession to me.

"That's not what we arranged," I said directly to her. "You said . . ."

"I know what had been previously arranged," Khadijah said. "This situation did not work out that way."

I took a deep breath. I kept my rage in check. I knew what an explosion could lead to. More antagonizing silence. More needless barriers.

We were helpless. Mati and I couldn't stay at the Dhaka Radisson Blue hotel forever. If we ever wanted to get back home to Florida, we had no choice but to play along.

Reluctantly, I agreed to go with them back to her house and got into their car.

The hour was already late when we arrived at Khadijah's family home. Traffic had been horrible, our slow pace only aggravating an already awkward situation.

The sky was getting dark as we moved silently to the front door. I sighed as Mati and I passed through, thinking, let's just get this charade over with.

Five agonizing hours came and went, spent in near silence as Khadijah and her family prepared for me to sign the affidavit. Nothing had been vetted because nothing had been drawn up to that point. I never let Mati out of my arms as they scrambled. Not for a second.

Khadijah hastily wrote a document that she was calling an affidavit. When I took a look at what she had written, even I could see that it amounted to little more than a letter. Nothing she wrote was official or legally binding.

Finally, after helping her come up with language for an affidavit that Khadijah felt comfortable with, I was eager to sign. All I wanted was to get back to the hotel with Mati to continue our time together. I had been more than patient dealing with this hand-wringing, and I made a point of outlining a small part of the absurdity I had gone through.

By now it was nearly midnight on Sunday. This was Mati and Daddy time.

Nabil, Khadijah, and her mother, Nargis, were clearly unfazed at the ridiculous amount of time this arduous process was taking. By now, I was beyond losing my patience.

I told Nargis this letter was clearly a case of blackmail, and everything about it was illegal. I told her and Khadijah I would sign whatever they wanted, if it would only allow me to get Mati and me on a plane as soon as possible. As far as I was concerned, the Bangladesh part of the war had come to a close. I would fight the next battle on American soil on another day.

Nargis erupted with fury, and an argument hastily ensued. Frightened, Mati began to panic, squirming and writhing in my arms.

Over and over, Nargis screamed for me to leave the boy. Someone forcibly grabbed Mati from my arms. She angrily ordered me to go back to the hotel and then get on the next flight home to the States. For the moment, I stood my ground and told her she had no rights to make such demands on us.

They threatened to call the police. They accused me of trespassing and abduction. Somehow, through all this fit of madness, I maintained an air of calm.

Mati was ushered away to another room. Alone, I was commanded once again to immediately return to my hotel. I had no choice. They prepared to make a call. Either I would walk away peacefully or be dragged out kicking and screaming. I chose the former.

I told them I would allow their Bangladeshi attorney to review the affidavit in hopes they would ultimately find it fraudulent and allow me to bring Mati home.

I left the apartment sobbing uncontrollably as Mati screamed out for me. The whole ride back to my hotel I continued weeping and sobbing.

Nabil sat beside me in the backseat. The driver's stoic eyes remained fixed on the road. I cried and wailed loudly, without shame. My cries were the only sound in the car.

I was out on a limb. I was halfway across the world and, for that short drive, I had nowhere and no one to turn to. I had never felt quite so alone as I did right then.

The car entered the hotel driveway, and my thoughts returned to a plan to keep Mati and I together. I would not go down without a fight.

A few short moments earlier, I'd had Mati wrapped up in my arms, and now I was being forced farther away from him. With the lights of the hotel spire rising above the Dhaka skyline, I formed another way forward.

"Don't leave!" I shouted.

The driver glanced back as he pulled up to the hotel curb to drop me off. He looked to Nabil for what to do next.

"What are you talking about, Tyler?" Nabil asked.

"Do not leave," I said. "I'm going upstairs to my room to get my things."

Nabil shrugged.

As much as I had resented him for his role in all of this, I knew he was an almost powerless figure. Much like I had been, Nabil was a pawn in Khadijah's game of control.

I could tell he had been relieved when I finally let Mati out of my grasp. Now I was forcing him back into the fire.

"You heard me," I said with one foot out the door.

"Why?"

"I'm going to get my suitcase, and I'm going back to the house with you."

"Have you thought this through, Tyler?"

"I won't leave his side," I said. "Now wait here."

I watched Nabil gesture calmly to the driver. In that moment, I could have sworn he was instructing him to stay put and wait.

I ran as fast as I could through the lobby. In the elevator I checked out my reflection. I was a tear-streaked mess, sallow and pale, wan with exhaustion. I gritted my teeth, showing myself a show of strength and fortitude.

I sprinted for my room door and slid my key through the lock. Ever since I had checked in, I had decided it would be best to keep my bags packed at all times in case of moments like this one where I wanted to be ready to move at the drop of a hat.

With suitcase now in hand, I ran back down the staircase when the elevator took too long to arrive on my floor. Through the lobby, I staggered out to the drop-off where I expected to find Nabil and the driver in an idling car.

The car was gone. Nabil and the driver were nowhere inside the hotel gate. Frantically, I raced through the parking lot and out to the road to see if I could catch them

They were nowhere to be found.

I curled into a ball in the fetal position at the foot of my hotel bed. I could not bring myself to crawl in and sleep. The sounds outside dulled until I could no longer hear the city.

Waves of nausea came and went through me. Each passing one seemed to mount with an increasing intensity until I could stand it no longer. I moved to the bathroom where I sprawled out on the cold tile floor at the base of the toilet and shower.

Mati had been in my arms. He had been so close to me, only to be gone. If the car ride home had been my low point up till that moment, I had reached a new, much darker valley.

My phone sat on the nightstand by the bed. It was full of messages, mostly from my mother and father who had not heard from me in a long time. I even had a message from Hans. I could not listen to those voices. The feeling of loss and defeat was far more than I could bear telling anyone without falling apart.

For the moment, I was too weak to scheme. I was too drawn out to even talk.

My fatigue did not last forever, though. On the tear-soaked floor of that hotel room, I sat up and slowly began to jot down a few notes, ideas, whatever thoughts came to mind.

Then my ideas came in a more fluid flow. I felt myself regaining control over the situation and my precarious place in it. When I felt strong enough, I called Hans in his room.

"Do you have anything today?" I asked.

"Nothing I cannot cancel. What happened, Tyler?" he asked. Hans knew I had gone to Khadijah's house, and he sounded relieved to hear my voice. I felt good to have him close by.

When we met ten minutes later at our usual spot by the hotel pool, we embraced.

I told him my entire story up to the night before, sparing no detail. All of the shame and anger I had felt for letting him go the night before had already evaporated.

Hans had been an entrepreneur for most of his career. He had traveled extensively in international circles and worked in business ventures all around the world. As we resumed our conversation, this time in a more strategic manner, these were some of our touchstones.

Hans was a friend, but he was also a resource.

What became very helpful to me was that Hans had been working in and around Southeast Asia, and particularly Bangladesh, for a number of decades. He had made a name for himself in the textile industry working with factory owners there since the late 1980s when the area reopened for trade. When it came right down to it, Hans knew pretty well how the country worked inside and out.

Politically, Bangladesh, a country still struggling to develop an adequate infrastructure, operated quite differently than the United States. Their government could best be classified as a parliamentary-style democracy. With less oversight, corruption is far more rampant, more blatant than even in the worst American cities. In Bangladesh, to get anywhere, bribes and dirty money greased the wheels better than being on the right side of the law. What further complicated my attempts to maneuver legally was that Bangladesh was still not a signatory to the Hague Convention. That meant they would not automatically uphold a legal order from an American court.

As I soon learned of that critical abstention, I had the sinking realization that I would be forced to double every one of my legal efforts. Whatever documentation I had in place already in America, I would have to work to get in place, or at least legally recognized, in Bangladesh.

As Hans and I spoke, the best plan we could come up with was making preliminary contact with the United States Embassy in Dhaka. An embassy serves as a diplomatic mission to represent citizens travelling abroad. Hans explained to me that whenever one of his American consultants or employees had trouble, that was the first place he would advise them to go.

From whatever angle we attempted to look at my increasingly ambiguous legal situation, all roads seemed to lead there.

Khadijah and I finally got the chance to speak on the phone. Our conversation was, understandably, brief and terse.

She informed me that her lawyers had told her the affidavit we had worked so hard on for all those hours held no power whatsoever. They informed her and her family that it would never hold up in a court of law. Still, though, they would not bring Mati to me. We had wasted all of our time bickering, and now we had arrived at what seemed like an insurmountable impasse.

I called the American embassy. I told whoever would listen to me about the horrors and blatant injustice of my situation. I was an American citizen, my rights had been grossly violated, and I demanded that someone pay attention and take action to end my plight.

I called Paul Roquant, my family attorney back home in Naples. Over the years, Paul had become a strong legal ally, as well as one of my closest friends. He would surely prove a strong advocate for my fight to get Mati back. Paul agreed to back my play when it was time to make it.

The time for confrontation with Khadijah had long gone. She could curse and stonewall me for as long as she felt justified, and I didn't have that kind of patience. I knew I had some hard work to do, and I formed an ad hoc team with whomever I could strategize with on what those next steps should be.

First, I would have to make a motion in the US court. What I was seeking was referred to as my "sole legal and physical custody" of Mati, a designation that required me to apply for an emergency passport. I would be able to secure that document through the embassy in Dhaka.

However, in order to get that passport, I would need to have a current photo of Mati and other notarized paperwork. I pleaded about the obvious obstacle. In order to get a current photograph, I had to have my son, and at the moment, I would have had an easier time getting my hands on anything else under the sun besides him.

Many of the people at the embassy proved helpful and informative. During each of our numerous interactions, they assured me I had covered all my bases. They could not, however, provide me with what I needed more than anything else: I needed to somehow get Mati in person to the embassy for them to issue an emergency passport and subsequent exit visa to get us out of the country. Affirmations were nice, but good feelings were nowhere near my goal.

My second track had to be securing a professional mediator to sort out the complicated parental agreement that had so severely gone off track. As long as Khadijah and her family held Mati's passport, it was a proxy to holding the boy hostage. I had to arrange for some sort of agreement that would allow me a quicker solution than what had become a hostile negotiation.

I had worked with Holly Chernoff a few times before. Holly was known as one of the most respected mediators back in Naples. When I finally got her on the phone, out of bed in the middle of the night, she was happy to resume work on our case. Holly and I began to communicate frequently over Skype. I sent her every document and paper I had collected. We had marathon calls at all hours of the day and night.

She was always forthcoming with me, which was one of the traits I appreciated most about working with her. Holly explained that it was clear to her, and to any other objective person looking at this case, that on all sides I was being blackmailed and that I had been from the beginning of the process. Our written so-called agreement was dangerously one-sided. The document's sole purpose was to effectively keep Mati in Bangladesh through his college years. Again, affirmation was a satisfying but cold proposition.

I finally got a small sense of relief, however. I was far out on a limb but not outside of the law. In absentia, the US Court approved my motion for sole legal and physical custody of Mati, and they demanded that we all return to the courtroom in the United States.

Dates were set for us to meet in US court at the end of the summer. These were demands I would be happy to meet, but I doubted that Khadijah would reciprocate.

With the courts now firmly on my side, I decided I could press Khadijah where I felt it would hurt the most. I would press her shield and source of protection, her family.

I sat down and composed a long and detailed email message in which I described the situation regarding my attempt to bring Mati home for our agreed-upon time.

I wrote out, loud and clear, every single detail I thought to be relevant. I held nothing back. I titled my document "Summary of Events in Dhaka 07/12/2014 through 07/21/2014."

I addressed the letter to her older brother and sister, who I felt were the last remaining members of her family I could trust.

Greetings, Porag and Nasreen,

Here is the accurate summary of events in my attempt to get Mati so far.

I started the letter where my concern was greatest, with Mati's welfare.

As soon as I arrived in Dhaka, I went to Khadijah's house. I had no interest in their offer to eat lunch together or exchange any other pleasantries. I told your sister I had a driver waiting and I only came to get Mati and return to my hotel.

During this time, I noticed that Mati had two open wounds—one on his knee and another on his elbow. A bruise over his right eye was blackened slightly. I figured these were from general horseplay and nothing else. However, it concerned me that the wounds were not bandaged, so that night I put Band-Aids and antibiotics on his wounds.

In spite of everything, we had a magical reunion, and I was relieved to discover that there was no love lost over the eleven months that Khadijah had kept Mati from me.

I pressed further. I gave Khadijah's brother and sister solid details, likely their first view as to how Khadijah was blocking any reasonable attempts at a reunion with Mati.

The following day, I invited Khadijah and Nabil to the hotel. The only way Khadijah would provide me with Mati's passport was if I signed an affidavit that absolved her of violations of the parenting agreement over the past two years. In addition, she wanted me to agree to pay for all of her court costs and any travel expenses if I ever took her to court.

Realizing this was the only way I could get Mati out of the country, I was willing to sign anything, and said that I wanted to do so immediately. For weeks prior to my arrival, I begged her to provide me with a list of her terms and demands, but so far, she had not.

Mati and I had no interest of leaving with her from the hotel the following day. Mati said he just wanted to go to Florida.

"Let's go," he said, "I want to see Grammy and Grandpa Woody!"

However, Khadijah insisted that since both of her fathers were "dying" that Mati needed to say some final good-byes and get his clothes and toys packed before leaving. My hands were tied.

Once we returned to her parents' house, she broke out the old parenting agreement and attempted to make modifications. She also started typing out the affidavit that she was requiring I sign before she would provide me with Mati's passport.

After three hours of waiting and repeated attempts and requests from Mati that he wanted to go, she insisted that we finish the affidavit. She did not get us Mati's toys or clothes. It was now 12 a.m. on Sunday night, and she said that until we got this affidavit reviewed by her attorney, she would not allow me to leave her parents' home with Mati. If I attempted to go to my hotel, she would call the police. I immediately told everyone that I felt VERY uncomfortable and that Mati and I were being held against our will.

I felt I should get out of the house immediately, yet she would not allow Mati and me to leave. Eventually I had no choice, and I told Mati I had to go but he needed to stay. Mati immediately began to cry. He pleaded, saying he did not want to leave my side.

All of this upheaval was traumatic for him after not seeing me for eleven months. Although we were only together for one night before, Mati told me every thirty minutes he loved me and that he never wanted to leave my side again.

After further describing the circumstances and some of the needless court proceedings that followed, I brought the letter to a close.

During the time Khadijah and Mati were together, she finally noticed that his wounds had become infected. She asked me what I thought it was and what she should do about it.

I told Khadijah to go and see a doctor. I was firm, though, in saying that a few wounds were not a valid excuse for keeping Mati away from me. This story had been fabricated later on as a convenient excuse for not bringing Mati to the embassy so officials there could verify his well-being as a US citizen and minor child living abroad. I had been attempting to bring Khadijah to the embassy to talk freely with Sharon Weber in order to resume my parenting time with Mati, as Khadijah had been holding Mati hostage from me for over a week and counting.

After meetings with the US Embassy, the inspector general of the Bangladesh Police, calls with a Bangladesh FBI chief, and the local news stations, I feel that not only is the truth on my side, but the laws here in Bangladesh are as well. I have notified Khadijah of the sole custody court order demanding she return Mati to me, but again, she has not responded.

I have copied her entire family on this letter. I addition, I have copied officials at the State Department that are handling my case, as they have started the process of directly contacting the inspector general of police and the Bangladesh child services.

Sincerely,
Tyler Wood

The vehemence of my writing felt quite clear. I used the simplest language I could to describe what I had seen and what I had gone through since Khadijah had blatantly broken our court-ordered parenting agreement.

My rights were not a speculative matter anymore. This situation had become serious. They needed to act and act fast because I was coming for him.

Hans and I began to work on a few of his local connections at the same time. He had contacts with the local bureau of investigation in Dhaka, what amounted to the Bangledeshi FBI. He also had many high-level friends, and every one of them got a phone call as well. We felt the more people that knew my story, the better it would be for us.

We had turned up the heat a notch and had to continue. I developed a small media relations team and we worked tirelessly, from every angle we could, to leverage some press attention onto our situation. We wanted to get the media on our side, to fight our fight on the news or Internet, whatever might cause enough of a stir to draw Khadijah out of hiding.

Hans was instrumental in keeping my mood high and focused squarely on the goal.

"Go with the truth," he said.

This was good advice.

"At least while it's on your side, right?" he would continue. "All my life, I've learned that only criminals fear the light of day."

We were in the light, I felt. The longer we stayed here, the better.

We hammered our legal channels hard. We relentlessly petitioned the Bangladeshi courts to acknowledge our US-drawn agreements. Anyone looking could see that my rights had been violated, but the process was slow and often noncommunicative. We would make a motion and not hear back for days and weeks. Working against indifference was exhausting.

In a bold show of strength, I confronted a high-profile Bangladeshi police officer. I had quite an entourage at my side as I stormed into his station and demanded that he and his officers help me get Mati back.

For as good as it felt to rail against the machine, we did not get as far as we wanted. All we did was make a little noise. Everything we did seemed to return us to a square one.

Within a few short days of my lowest ebb, the wheels finally began to turn. Progress was slow, however, and I was missing one critical piece: I had not seen Mati since I'd let him go.

My visa was dangerously close to running out. So I decided I would set up my base of operations nearby in Thailand. A quick flight ran regularly either out of Bangkok or Phuket. I could be in Dhaka in a matter of hours if anything broke my way.

I found a cheap, comfortable apartment on Airbnb located in Phuket and got acquainted with the island. Online, I reconnected with most of my client base and was able to remain somewhat productive in spite of being preoccupied with my struggle.

Being able to speak the language of work proved to be therapeutic, distracting my mind from the gloomy situation in which I was teetering helplessly.

Phuket is a comfortable island, small and easy to navigate. I did not go out much. I focused all of my angst on improving my body. I exercised day and night and resumed my yoga practice. I ran on the beaches. I did marathon sets of push-ups and sit-ups on my apartment floor until I collapsed. At times, I felt as though I were training for a heavyweight fight. This fight was proving to be a marathon, not a sprint, and endurance became a prime objective. I had to be in prime physical condition to overcome whatever obstacle came next.

No matter how hard I worked my body, though, I often did not sleep well at night. I had trouble falling asleep and once there, had trouble staying. During this time, I often found myself alone and focusing hard on my goals regardless of the time of day or night.

My parents and friends stayed in close contact, but maintaining relationships proved to be quite a difficult chore. In a logistical sense, the time difference was difficult to overcome. Home was half a world away. Communicating everything that I was going through all the time was depressing as well. Sometimes it proved easier to stay alone, bottled up, conserving energy.

I looked into a long list of family law practitioners with practices located in Dhaka. For a while, I was tempted to throw good money after bad to retain a high-powered legal firm and go at her from this angle, but I never pulled the trigger.

A few times I strategized about hiring my own SWAT team to follow Mati and snatch him off the playground at school. It was a scene out of a thriller. Sure, he would be frightened, but only momentarily before he would not have to be frightened anymore. Taking the law into my own hands felt like an empowering step, but when I thought long and hard about all that went into such a plan, it flew in the face of Hans's best advice: Keep the law on my side.

When I got stressed out, I did yoga and meditated to keep a positive mental attitude. I left Thailand and for a short time visited my childhood best friend and his family in Singapore. He had been doing well in the stem cell industry, and I needed to feel the comfort of our close friendship. He had a beautiful family, and the time I spent with everyone proved to be a blessing.

While I was working diligently with Hans and his connections, Khadijah remained cold. She kept me at a distance. I tried every avenue I could think of to communicate with her. We never spoke throughout the summer. We only infrequently shared a few words through email and via text. I tried to arrange for supervised visits with Mati. We told her that we could meet at the safety of the American embassy. I wanted desperately to at least gain some knowledge about his physical and emotional well-being, but I was stonewalled. They would not bring him under any circumstances, perhaps an unintended consequence of the letter I had sent to out her entire family; I would never know. They always said he was in school or had taken ill or was otherwise indisposed with some activity and could not come see me.

Two or three times over that whole summer they conceded to let us talk. They would put Mati in a room, on Skype, but our conversations were brief. We only shared a few words, and his answers were obviously guarded and coached.

One of my worst fears was realized through those conversations. Nothing about him seemed natural. I hardly recognized my own son.

Anyone could see that he was a sad and brokenhearted little boy who had been placed in the cage of Khadijah's selfish and illegal actions. Everyone in her family was complicit in this.

We did whatever we could to enjoy our time together online. He played with toys, showing me what he liked and what he did with the family. Sometimes he would show off his favorite games.

He asked how his Grammy and Grandpa were, and I told him they loved him and were thinking of him every day.

I never discussed the custody ordeal with Mati. It crossed my mind, but on the subject of my fight with his mother, I remained mute.

Although we both undeniably felt the weight of the elephant in the room, I thought it best to keep the tone of our conversations optimistic and fun.

However awkward, I felt I accomplished something in those calls. I simply wanted my son to get used to the idea of connecting and talking to his real father again.

For what it was worth, we did. I could only hope he felt something too.

• • •

August came fast upon us, and the time on my work and travel visa had almost run out. Soon I would have to be back in the United States. I packed my things and prepared.

The realization that I was not going to be bringing Mati along on this flight home with me as I had envisioned was heartbreaking. I did my best to ignore the feeling and to continue thinking positively, but the effort was almost too much.

I said good-bye to Phuket and Thailand, but I somehow knew I would be back soon.

A court order to return to the United States was issued for our upcoming hearing, but Khadijah remained steadfast in her defiance. She threw up a wall, even in the face of what seemed like objective reality.

At this juncture, I expected nothing but nasty from her. And that was what I got. "I hope those pieces of paper from America bring you comfort," she messaged me over Skype.

I had not gotten Mati back, but the cracks in her facade were beginning to show. I could hang some pride on at least this much.

Khadijah's family was obviously running out of patience by now. They were embarrassed by Khadijah's actions, and every one of them pined for an end to this ordeal as well. They knew I was a loving, devoted father but had no control in the face of Khadijah's selfishness.

I could not say that the tide of opinion had shifted in my favor, but for the first time in what felt like a long while, we were bringing the fight to them and she did not like it one bit.

• • •

When I returned to Naples, I was reunited with my family. Everyone seemed aware that my return was for a single purpose. We anxiously awaited for our hearing date. We all had the date September 9th circled on the calendar.

The questions ran rampant. Would Khadijah show up in court to defend herself? And if she did, would she bring Mati with her?

As the day drew closer, I became nervous, but one thing kept me buoyed. As Hans had said, and I continued to remind myself, I had the law on my side.

The hearing was a complete and total no-show. I suppose we were foolish to ponder any other end. Khadijah never showed up. She never even called in to defend herself by phone. All of the court's generous offers to her to Skype in and plead her case went unanswered.

She did not even bother to hire a stateside attorney to represent her. She was now, as she had for the entire time up until that point, choosing contempt. She would ignore the bigger problem rather than address it with anything resembling maturity.

The judge was tough on Khadijah. In the end, she was charged with criminal contempt of court, a judgment that she was notified of via email. When the time came to read out her sentence, the judge gave her 365 days in jail. One whole year in prison was what she ended up getting for all the harm she had done to Mati and me.

On one hand, her penalty seemed stiff. On the other hand, it seemed entirely warranted.

We had scored a resounding victory. We finally had a reason to celebrate. But it was a pale feeling. A victory in Naples gave us no momentum overseas.

My family and I were still without Mati.

Whether Khadijah served any of that time in jail did not matter to me in the least. Although the judge had ordered her to return Mati back to me in Naples with all of his possessions and legal documents in hand, she was not present to turn him or his things over.

We were, once again, on the right side of an international legal stalemate.

With this victory now well in hand, we still had so much more to do. We needed to find some means of breaking Khadijah's stranglehold.

Hans and I spoke that night. I described our Naples trial to him. I told him how lonesome I still was. Although Hans congratulated me, we both knew that what we had did not amount to an endgame.

The ruling had come without a measure of finality.

I knew I had to return to Bangladesh. The next day, I sent Hans a copy of everything I had and planned my next flight overseas.

CHAPTER 7

• • •

AT THIS JUNCTURE, NOTHING COULD be left to chance. The timing of my return trip to Bangladesh was meticulously planned. I had coordinated my arrival to a date and time when I knew Hans would be there as well.

Over the last few months, Hans had been invaluable to me for how well he was acquainted with the delicate ins and outs of working in Bangladesh. He knew life on the ground. What would become far more valuable on this critical trip, however, was how well he knew critical people that I simply could not get access to.

One of Hans's closest associates in Bangladesh was a man named Zahid. Hans and Zahid had worked together for many years and had grown quite close, developing a relationship that was more of a friendship. Hans manufactured textiles in a series of interconnected factories that he and his partners owned. They spoke the language of everyday Bangladeshi people. Zahid could talk to people in a way I simply could not.

My arrival in Dhaka was unceremonious. Once I was safely on the ground, we began working on our plan, as I had only been afforded a limited time on my visa.

Soon after arriving, Hans and I booked a direct flight from Dhaka to Chittagong. A major manufacturing hub located on the southeast coast of Bangladesh on the Bay of Bengal, near the eastern delta of the Ganges-Brahmaputra river, Chittagong is the second largest city in the country and the major international shipping port of the country. Even with a metro area pressing to nearly seven million people, the city feels a signifi-cant step slower than Dhaka.

I was an honored guest of Hans and Zahid. They introduced me into their world and treated me like a traveling dignitary. Before long, Zahid and his colleagues acted more like brothers to welcome me into their cir-cle. They went out of their way to make me feel comfortable. Before set-tling down to the delicate business of getting Mati back, they took me on an extensive tour of their factories and showed me the inner workings of their operations.

What I learned upon meeting Zahid was that members of his family were well connected in the local political scene, as well as on the ground in business. Zahid's father-in-law was an acting member of parliament, which gave him invaluable access to the system. Our first order of busi-ness was to create a legal team that we could base out of Dhaka. Back home in Naples, I had two lawyers working behind the scenes. They were the best I could find and were both good friends. Paul Roquant worked as my family attorney, and Ted Hudgins was the man I trusted to safeguard the money in his escrow account for wiring emergency funds. However, in Bangladesh, I would need operatives who worked within this specific sys-tem and were comfortable in the wildly different environment.

Initially, we set up a meeting with a team of attorneys that the family recommended. We sat down and took a few hours in the evening to tell them our story, and after showing them our mountains of paperwork, they quoted us their fee for handling the case.

I was shocked by the amount, and by the look of my cooperatives on either side of me, they were taken aback as well.

As they waited for our response, Zahid pulled Hans and me back.

In spite of the obvious complexity of my case, the amount of money these lawyers were asking for was exorbitant.

"Something about this whole setup just doesn't feel right," Zahid said.

Hans and I agreed. My gut told me the same thing. The price these lawyers were asking for was tantamount to price gouging. They saw my precarious situation and seized on it as their opportunity to milk what they believed to be a rich foreigner for every cent they possibly could. I was vulnerable. This felt like extortion.

Perhaps they would have proven to be an effective legal team, I will never know. At that cost, however, I risked using up all the money I had in reserve before I even had Mati in my hands.

We returned to the room and turned them down flat.

I was disappointed, but that feeling didn't linger for long. Of course, Zahid had a few tricks up his sleeve, as he would prove to time and again. Not long after we walked out of that conference, we moved into Plan B.

As our first choice proved too expensive, Zahid's thoughts had drifted to another option, a person he trusted deeply back in Chittagong.

"It is very good synergy that I thought of him," he said.

Zahid told us about a previous working associate he stayed in close contact with, a man named Rafeek. Many years ago, Rafeek had worked for Zahid as an employee, helping run one of his many textile factories. After he was done working those long and difficult days, he bettered himself, studying to become an attorney while attending classes at a local night school. He was a hardworking, self-made man, precisely the kind of person we were seeking.

Most important, though, Zahid could vouch for him. He was smart. Rafeek had keen attention to detail, and according to Zahid, he was someone we could rely on under fire.

Without knowing if he was available or not, Zahid called out to his old friend and asked to set up a meeting. Our hope was that he could take on my case at a more reasonable rate than we had just been quoted. Lucky for us, Rafeek agreed to meet without hesitation.

"Anything for a friend of Zahid," he said.

Meeting with Rafeek proved to be the right move. Zahid was right about the element of synergy. Rafeek fit seamlessly into our team.

After our meeting, Rafeek became my quarterback attorney in Bangladesh.

From this point forward, my role transformed. I moved into a more hands-off capacity. Everything logistical would run through Zahid and Rafeek. They arranged for plane tickets when we needed to move around. They hired all of my Supreme Court attorneys. Rafeek oversaw the work of the people we hired, monitoring them for efficacy. I was free to become the face of this struggle.

Rafeek offered what proved to be sage advice about money and how we should handle it while in Bangladesh. He told us, whatever we did, not to talk about money. We were to leave any matters of money for him to negotiate. Odds were, anyone that saw me would presume I was a rich foreigner and would take the opportunity to try and gouge a sucker as the previous attorneys had.

For this process to work, I had to place my absolute trust in Rafeek's hands. And I did, almost without reservation. Fate had led me to meet Hans on that Radisson Blue pool deck. My relationship with Hans had led me to a fast friendship with Zahid, and Zahid had led me to Rafeek. Everything had seemingly fallen into place.

When Zahid mentioned synergy, the idea resonated with me. My future with my son was dangling precariously in the balance, and from now on, I was in their capable hands.

Money would be an ongoing issue, so I felt relieved to hand over the reins of that responsibility to Rafeek. I had a war chest socked away for the fight.

Back home in Naples, my attorney Ted Hudgins was holding thirty-five thousand dollars for me in his law firm's bank account. These were my funds for operations. When I needed to get my hands on any money, I would call Ted, and the plan was that he would wire it to me.

Before I left for Bangladesh, we worked out a code word. We needed something I could pass along to him to prove that my request was not being made under duress.

After some deliberation, the code word we decided on was "marathon."

A chain would form from that code word out. Rafeek and Zahid would do the work behind the scenes. Whenever they needed more money, Zahid would contact me and I would contact Ted. Every time I got in a car or on a plane, filed paperwork, or hired a new member of the team, Rafeek was at the decision-making helm that pulled the trigger on cash.

A few days into my trip, all the tasks were delegated. Everyone knew what was at stake. It was time to make our first move. Time would prove to be a factor as much as money.

Everyone on my team knew we were under the gun and had to work fast. I was only in Bangladesh on a thirty-day visa. I had less than one month to introduce and move my delicate multinational case through a foreign government's unpredictable parliamentary legal system. I was far from home and didn't speak the language, but I was no longer alone.

One of the primary roadblocks that stood between Mati and me was convincing the Bangladeshi court that the documents and agreements created earlier in the US courts were valid. This finding would prove Khadijah culpable of breaking our parenting agreement. Without that acknowledgement, our contract and her violation of it, however airtight that may have seemed back home in Naples, Florida, wouldn't be worth the paper it was printed on here.

After hiring a few hand-chosen Supreme Court attorneys to back his initial play, Rafeek flew up from Chittagong to Dhaka to make that argument in front of a lower court. We had yet to reach the Supreme Court level, but everyone on my team was well aware that a favorable ruling here would have a positive effect of advancing our overall case.

The scene in that courthouse was bizarre. In some ways, stepping into those halls of law felt a bit like taking a trip back in time to a much older place.

The atmosphere was stuffy. Everyone who stepped forward to address the court wore formal black garments, like the governmental characters in some eighteenth-century drama.

Throughout the process, my anxiety level spiked. My stomach was bound up tightly in knots as the court worked down through the day's docket. Many hours passed before Rafeek and one of our Supreme Court attorneys was finally given his chance to stand before the presiding judge and present our argument.

My attorneys vehemently argued that the judge should validate our documents. Even if I could not speak the official legal language of Bengali, I saw in those first moments what Zahid had known all along about his former employee and friend. Rafeek was a passionate litigator. He was articulate, exuding confidence and a cool sense of control even when things were dire.

Although I could not quite bring myself to loosen my grip and relax, a sense of confidence began to take root in me. My case was in more than capable hands.

Ultimately, the judge agreed with our argument. He deemed that Khadijah had indeed been in direct violation with valid agreements. He decreed that she needed to turn Mati over to the court in Bangladesh for a proper hearing on the matter.

I maintained an even and outward demeanor as I heard that decision read to me, but inside, I could not help but celebrate our small victory. I was filled with joy as we embraced outside the courtroom.

We had taken a step toward getting Mati home, albeit a small one. We had gained momentum. As we left the building, the lawyers happily shook our hands. They encouraged us. They seemed proud of their work, what felt to them like a victory for justice.

My case had gained some valuable momentum, but the fact remained that I still had not seen my son in months. A father cannot hold a judge's decision. You cannot joke with it and make it laugh out loud. Clinging to the most recent pictures I had and my memories, I needed to be with him again

The next step was to assemble a plan to grab Mati. Rafeek worked to get us an audience with the local chief of police. If we were going to get a hand on Mati, we had to proceed carefully. And no doubt we could not move without some tactical support from the local police department.

I had no idea where Khadijah had been keeping Mati. I had the address to a residence I had culled from a few documents, but there was no telling whether Mati would be there when we knocked on the door or not. He could be living with her under her parents' protection. He could be staying with Nabil's family, wherever they were located. Mati could be anywhere in Dhaka, for all that we knew.

Everyone was in agreement with regards to timing. We would have one shot, and when we made it, it had to be right. We could not make a mistake or we would send up an alarm that we were making a move.

At the time, I may not have known where and with whom Mati was spending his nights, but I knew where he spent the majority of his days. Mati was enrolled in a special school. As we worked out our plan to grab him, I mentioned that he would likely be on campus every day.

Every single detail was considered. Each movement was carefully vetted. A few school security personnel would be on site, but with a police escort at the right time of day, we could extract the boy to a safe place with a minimum of drama or disruption. Every way we drew up our plan, going to his school proved to be a far cleaner option than his place of residence.

We decided to strike as soon as we were granted police escorts. Rafeek pushed even harder for an audience with the chief of police in the school's district, and once again, he made a convincing argument. The chief agreed. He would lend us a few uniformed and plainclothes cops to help us get Mati back.

If the earlier courtroom scenario had felt like an old-time drama, the next day's scene was pulled straight out of a modern-day thriller.

Around midmorning, we pulled up to a street across from the school. My young driver, Zihad, sat behind the wheel of the little van we used for transportation around Dhaka.

From the outside, we looked like anyone else. Inside, however, the air was heavy with tension. Beside me on one side sat Rafeek. On the other side sat one of my Supreme Court attorneys with our documents in hand.

We stared nervously out the windows, ready to spring into action on even the slightest movement. A small team of police officers waited nearby, ready to follow us inside when the time seemed right.

My stomach was bound up in knots once again. This anxiety was different, though. This time my tension was derived from excitement. I felt that I was mere moments away from seeing Mati again. I had already moved mountains to get this far. The time to reap my rewards was drawing ever closer.

Time passed. It felt like forever. I peered at the school from every angle to see if I could identify my son playing in the gated area around the school.

At first when we arrived, classes were still in session. The common area was quiet. Then the end-of-class bell rang out. I tensed further as the doors flew open. The children flooded the halls from their classrooms and moved around, laughing and playing.

This was the moment, but for an instant, Mati was nowhere in sight.

Then finally I saw him for a brief moment before he went back inside. I turned to the police, raised my hand in the air, and signaled. "I see him," I said. "It is time to make our move."

I watched as the uniformed men crossed the street toward the school's front doors. I waited for the signal that they were ready for me to follow. Everything seemed to be moving in slow motion as I waited for them to fan out into their prearranged tactical positions.

The lead officer nodded at me and waved his hand to say go ahead. I kept looking toward the hall where I expected to see Mati. But by then he had disappeared.

Khadijah's family had somehow found out that we were going to be there to get Mati. As we approached, he was secretly ushered out the back door of the school, into a waiting car.

Lucky for us, one of our plainclothes officers noticed a boy that he recognized as Mati from pictures and descriptions as he was hurried away toward a waiting car. Before they could take off and foil our plan altogether, he pulled his gun out and ordered them to stop.

We had believed that grabbing Mati at his school during the day would be easy, at least relatively easy. The hard part would come after he was with us.

Perhaps, in hindsight, my thinking had been a little naïve. I had allowed my optimism to override what should have been a sense of caution.

At this juncture, everything ground to a sudden and abrupt halt. Our precious momentum dissolved on the back steps of that school.

Unbeknownst to me, the hard part would begin right now.

Our officers had managed some brief communications with the school officials. After the confrontation behind the school, Mati had been ushered off to the local Police Department.

We felt good in spite of the confusion. This was the station where we had successfully lobbied the police chief. I was notified to follow them there. The sense of familiarity felt good.

Moments later, I arrived at the precinct station with my lawyers on both sides. I was uncertain of what I would find.

What I saw when I opened the door and entered the small, packed captain's office, however, should have been an expected outcome.

Mati and I saw each other for the first time. We were overjoyed to see each other again. However, Khadijah would not let him out of her clutches or let him even look at me. She kept trying to turn his head away from me. Her protectors, lawyers and family members, surrounded her for support. She held Mati tight and kept him from responding when I called out his name. I paid no attention to her and engaged Mati even though I was not able to hold him. We could touch each other and smile, knowing that I was back with him again.

Arguments raged back and forth. The worst outcome had come to life before our eyes. In effect, by trying to snatch Mati from his school, we had stepped on the tiger's tail.

Now Khadijah was furious and would not yield an inch.

All of her immediate family and their team of high-priced attorneys flanked her on all sides and argued vehemently with Rafeek and my attorneys about what came next.

I saw the developing scene for what it was. We had come so far, but now they were here and pushing back against us.

And what Khadijah and her family brought with them to the table amounted to an army.

The local police chief, only hours ago one of our allies, brought his officers awkwardly back into the office. I could sense immediately that something peculiar was going on. No matter how I provoked him, he would not make eye contact with me.

No matter how hard Rafeek pushed him or anyone else who would listen for an explanation for what was going on, he would not give us one. We were being stonewalled.

After quite a long time, Rafeek figured out that when the police chief had given his permission that morning, he had no idea who we had intended to spring from the school. In the chief's mind, my son could have been any other child. Now the chief was aware that Mati was a member of Khadijah's powerful family, and he abruptly closed the door on any further support for our cause as a result.

Had he known, we would have been run out of the station without a second look. Our hard-earned court documents went out the window. Khadijah's family was too influential. They were powerful enough to crush him, and as we would soon learn, they were wielding that influence, wherever and whenever they could to prevent Mati from ever getting close to me.

Rafeek pulled me aside after checking in with a few of his contacts. By this point, I was a frantic mess.

"Things are becoming tricky now," he said, concern written on his brow.

I didn't quite understand, but I trusted his judgment.

"Very tricky."

Rafeek never protected me by offering a watered-down version of what was happening. It was part of why I trusted him. He explained that Khadijah's family had started throwing large amounts of money around in the form of bribes. They had handsomely bribed the school precinct's police chief, forcing him to withdraw. They had also set the chief up with enough money to bribe every one of the officers that had only moments ago served as my protectors.

Rafeek looked at me dead in the eye when he explained that their river of dirty money had worked its way to our team as well. The scenario again seemed surreal. Under our noses, our Supreme Court attorneys had accepted their bribes in an attempt to undermine our efforts.

I found out later that even Rafeek had been offered fifty thousand dollars and his life was threatened.

We were teetering on a precarious edge. Who we were as a team had suddenly become quite flawed.

All of the time that we had been planning for Mati's rescue, we were well aware of the reality that we would eventually need more money in order to move the wheels of justice in our favor. This was one of the first truths that had been explained to me.

A large part of the parliamentary judicial system in Bangladesh ran on bribery and influence, and Khadijah's parents knew how and when to turn that on. Now that tide of influence was working against us, and it was clear they were very rich and powerful.

We gathered our composure and pushed back in any way we could.

Rafeek argued that we were sitting in the precinct that presided over Mati's school. After some thought, they agreed that a move would be appropriate. Slowly, we filed out of the small police station.

I hardly spoke as we drove across town. Rafeek and my remaining attorneys worked double time to make a strong play. I couldn't bring myself to say much.

We managed to move to a nearby station in Mati's home precinct. At that police station, Khadijah was forced to relinquish her grip. I had gotten lucky. She protested vehemently, screaming at anyone who came close to coax her, but finally, in those dingy hallways surrounded by enemies, Mati and I were allowed to be close to one another.

I held my son tight. We played together in the lobby. We snapped pictures on my phone and took a few silly videos to send back home to my worried parents. Here, under the most awkward of circumstances, my son and I reunited and managed to share a few magical moments. We had been robbed of our time together, but our love was never clearer.

"I want to go home to Florida and never come back," he said as I held him in my arms.

I had to get Mati out of there, at any cost. No matter how I pleaded my case with the police, though, they would not let Mati and me go back to my hotel.

I was certainly free to go there alone, they said, but under no circumstances would we be allowed to go there together. They were steadfast in this decision.

Outside of those station doors, we would be on our own, without any protection whatsoever. I decided it was best to simply stay put.

Rafeek worked tirelessly as the day wore on. He offered me a few details, whenever he saw fit and I was available to listen. The family had brought guns for hire into the fold, he explained, and they were ready to use them. The other Supreme Court lawyers on our team were frightened, unsure of what to do next.

As we lingered in the station, Zahid called me on the phone late that evening.

"We need more money, Tyler," he said. "And we need it now."

Since our failed snatch-and-grab at the school, our situation was becoming increasingly delicate. All the bribes that Khadijah's family had spread around were making it difficult for us to maneuver. Somehow, he said, we had to try and compete with their money.

It was midday for Ted Hudgins back in Naples when I messaged him urgently with our secret password to send more money immediately.

As soon as I gave him the code word marathon, the money transfer was put in motion. I imagined that somewhere, through silent back channels and wires, my money was finding its way to Zahid, who was still operating in the shadows.

All I could do was cling to Mati, calm myself, and wait patiently. I had to avoid becoming too cynical and keep my hopes up.

That was becoming, however, an increasingly difficult proposition.

It was the middle of the night in Dhaka, yet all around us, the halls and conference rooms were bustling with the comings and goings of legal activity. The police precinct never rested. The appearance of justice was a twenty-four-hour business in Bangladesh.

We had all reached a precarious point far beyond exhaustion. Our bodies began to give out a little, even if our vigilance remained in a heightened state.

Khadijah and Nabil lingered nearby. They would not allow Mati and me out of their sights for even a single second. If one got up to use the toilet, the other's eyes were peeled.

When I got hungry, Rafeek brought me whatever food he could find at that hour. It was awful. Not even extreme hunger could compel me to take a second bite.

If either Mati or I needed a drink of water, someone would run and fetch it. I wouldn't turn my back for any reason. The stalemate was wicked.

Mati would not let go of me. Worn out from the emotions of the ordeal, he hung from my body, his little arms wrapped tightly around the back of my neck.

We had remained attached throughout the night, yet somehow I managed to maintain the endurance to keep him there. Anytime a lawyer, police officer, or Khadijah would try to touch him or coax him away from me even for a moment, he fought back viciously, screaming at them. There was no reasoning with him. Only there in my arms was he peaceful.

This was the way we slept, or at least tried to sleep. I sat on a small chair with Mati curled up on me. Khadijah stayed too. She slept in a chair down the row next to Nabil.

The scene was bizarre, all of us together—another in a series of moments that was difficult to comprehend. So much time apart, scheming on how to one-up the other, yet we now found ourselves in the same room. We hardly spoke to each other. The tension was too intense to penetrate with words.

Somewhere in the early morning hours, sheer exhaustion got the better of me. Mati and I had fallen into a hard sleep.

Neither of us heard her move.

Khadijah got up from her seat and crept slowly across the room toward us and grabbed Mati away from me.

As she hurried toward Nabil, Mati awoke. As he realized the situation, he reached desperately over her shoulder in my direction. I went for his hand. I grabbed at his fingers for dear life. She twisted and dodged, breaking our grip whatever way she could.

"Daddy, pull me!" Mati screamed. "Take me, Daddy, please!"

Again I reached out and grabbed his hand. Our bodies tangled together.

Khadijah hissed at me in front of the police officers. We shouted back and forth, making furious claims about what Mati wanted. She claimed that the boy wanted to be with her family instead of mine, in spite of what anyone could clearly see were his demands.

The police responded to break up the ruckus. She said that I had attacked her. She claimed that I, in a blind fury, had tried to hurt her and my son. As she had before in our Naples condo, Khadijah had become desperate and saw her only option to make false accusations.

Regardless of how preposterous Khadijah's claim might have been, it forced me back into a corner. The most ludicrous aspect of her claims was that they had to be taken seriously.

The police officers ushered Khadijah and a screaming, sobbing Mati away into another room. By now, I had reached my breaking point. I demanded that we be given a hearing. I was tired, completely overwhelmed by the ordeal of the last twenty-four hours.

Our best course of action would be in the courts, and I insisted that we be given our chance at a fair hearing. A few hours later, at eleven a.m., we were brought before a judge.

The courtroom was packed to the walls with attorneys and members of Khadijah's family. Other benches were full of bystanders waiting for their own hearings.

Under this microscope, Rafeek introduced me for the first time to my team of newly hired Supreme Court attorneys. These were new guys, still unbribed by her family's wide web of influence. They seemed sharp enough as we discussed the few specifics we had the time to review, but reality was, they had only been brought onto the case the night before.

They assured me they had a grasp of what was going on. Once again, I had no choice but to trust that their claim was true.

Khadijah entered the courtroom. I was allowed to see my son again. Mati and I were kept far apart through the preliminary aspect of the trial, but I could see that he was visibly upset and confused. Khadijah would keep turning Mati's face away from being able to look in my direction.

Besieged on all sides, I took my place before the judge. As my lawyers addressed the court, I had no choice but to let go and allow the process to run its course.

Once again, I found myself at the center of a scene so surreal that it still feels oddly like a work of fiction. Here I was, a stranger halfway around the world, pitted against power and corruption, petitioning for my son.

Outside, people passing by the courtroom stared in through the windows. Their peering eyes made it feel like we were on the set of a television program. Unbeknownst to me, our custody case had built into a local scandal. Everyone seemed to know what was going on and was curious about all of the light being shined on this particular hearing.

Being high profile, Khadijah's family had done everything they could to keep this dirty custody fight out of the public eye. Khadijah's antics were a shame when revealed to the public. From the looks of how things were shaping up, her family was slowly losing that fight.

The scene those passersby caught a glimpse of was one of pure chaos. The case was argued in a bitter mix of Bengali and English, which I could not help but believe was sprinkled in for my benefit. One moment I knew what was going on, and the next, I could not understand a single word of what was being said. My only consistent gauge was to read the expressions on faces and body language to try and ascertain what was going on.

Since Rafeek had revealed the level of bribery and corruption that we were up against, I had made numerous calls to the US Embassy in Dhaka.

I told them I needed a witness, someone from their office in an official capacity to come in and watch as an American citizen was systematically losing his rights. This was an outrage.

I had spent a night in prison. My attorney, when a bribe was not accepted, was threatened with murder. My son was being withheld. I needed help.

They were aware that this trial was taking place. As I looked back into the sea of faces, I realized that the US Embassy had indeed come through to help. They sent two people to witness the court proceedings, one who was fluent in Bengali.

Gradually, I noticed the lawyers were speaking less and less in English. They had reverted back to their native Bengali to really drive their points home.

Eventually, I lost my tenuous grip on what was happening. Rafeek's look was harder to gauge with each twist and turn. My other lawyers, arguing for my life, were complete strangers, leaving me at a loss for what might be going through their minds.

What came next dropped like a bomb in our laps. My hands curled into fists as I heard Khadijah's attorneys introduce a new argument. They said that Mati was not an American citizen at all.

Instead, her team made the case that he was, in fact, a Bangladeshi citizen. Since Mati currently carried a passport issued in Bangladesh, it logically meant that he did not have the concurrent rights of a United States citizen.

The implication of their argument was clear. If this were found to be the decision by the court, our American legal documents would add up to nothing.

My team of lawyers was blown away. No more English was spoken at any point, only a rapid, frantic Bengali, bandied between dramatic hand gestures and other histrionics. The lawyers were sparring hard, shouting back and forth before the judge rose from his bench.

Then, like a curtain, the arguments dropped to silence. I looked around. The courtroom had drawn to an eerie standstill.

Rafeek stood back. I read relief in his eyes. He winked as the judge called both legal teams into his private chambers. He wanted to discuss the case away from the gallery of faces. As the bailiffs closed the doors, voices suddenly coursed back throughout the room.

I had been left behind with a single attorney at my side. Far across the room, Mati sat facing away from me. Khadijah shielded his gaze from mine. She was braced with humiliation. The pressure was on her, too. The way I saw it, she had no right to keep him from me.

I told my attorney to argue that Mati had a right to sit with me. Without hesitation, he stood out of his chair and argued with the nearest official. He pointed at me and demanded that Mati sit on my side of the aisle, that the boy had the right to be reunited with his father. Until compelled otherwise by the court, I had rights equal to hers that could not be withheld.

Lucky for me, they agreed. In front of the packed house and all those ogling bystanders, a couple of officers eased Mati out of her arms and brought him across to me. Khadijah could not pitch another fit of false accusations like she had at the station, not under this heat and pressure.

She quietly let Mati go.

Once again, Mati and I were brought back together. Our reunion was no less emotional. Just as he had back in the police station, Mati took hold of me and would not let go.

We took some deep breaths. I felt him slowly calm.

The attorneys emerged from the judge's chambers after what felt like hours of deliberation. Each of them looked stern, minds racing under knitted brows and downcast eyes.

We were ordered to return with them to the judge's chambers. As we moved, Rafeek glanced over in my direction. He winked. He followed that with a strong look of assurance.

Although my attorney spoke no words, I knew we would at least survive this moment.

The judge slowly began to read his ruling to the silent room. Again, he spoke not a word of English, only Bengali. I glanced in Khadijah's direction and caught a glimpse of her weeping. The totality of our ordeal had made me callous. I felt nothing for her: no pity, no sympathy after all of the torture and humiliation she had put my family through over the last few years.

Rafeek nudged me. Once again, his expression told me that the results being read by the court were in our favor.

Mati and I would be granted six months together. But that was to be spent in Bangladesh, and Mati would not be permitted to leave the country under any circumstances.

During that period of six months, he would be given free access to Khadijah and members of her family. That lingering feeling of my needing to live in two worlds became a sudden possibility.

The judge also ordered that the case be moved into a family court. Family court, in Bangladesh, served as a kind of religious, Muslim-focused court where the case would be vetted on strictly moral grounds. In what felt like a last shot, Khadijah's family was also given the power to delay any future appeals on the matter for an inordinate amount of time. As it was explained to me, this could drag on for years on end without any further resolution.

Now all of the attention turned toward me. The decision whether to accept this fell on my shoulders. In private, Rafeek urged me to take the deal. We didn't have a lot of time.

With my full trust placed in him, I stepped forward. I was surrounded by strangers. When I was asked by that judge whether or not I agreed to the terms he had just described, I said that I did.

Then Rafeek stepped forward and demanded that in exchange for my compliance, I be granted a reasonable amount time to set up what would be my new life in Bangladesh. Our ordeal began with one person trapped in this foreign country against his will.

Now that I had agreed to this arrangement, there would be two.

The lawyers began to argue once again. For a fleeting moment, I disassociated and got lost in my own thoughts.

I was halfway around the world from Naples. Rafeek made the case that I needed sufficient time to set up housing and apply for an extension of my existing visa.

I snapped back in time to hear that the court had agreed. I would be given that time.

The way things would actually play out, I never set up any new housing in Bangladesh. Six months was not in the cards for us. I never extended my visa beyond what was set in a few days to expire. I said yes, but agreeing to these terms was part of a bigger plan.

Once we were out of that courtroom, my team would scramble to make another, much bolder move to get Mati home.

With a tentative agreement in place, we made the argument that Mati would stay with me as I made my transition to part-time life in Bangladesh. Considering how egregiously over-extended his stay with Khadijah and her family had been, the request for my taking immediate custody seemed quite reasonable.

Reluctantly, Khadijah's family agreed to these terms. In a sense, their hands had been tied. The hot light of public scrutiny was squarely focused on them. They didn't want any of that. What they needed more than anything else was for this whole ordeal to go away, and appearing graceful in granting me permission went a long way toward accomplishing that goal.

Now free to move with Mati, I was escorted by one of the police officers. I was ordered to head directly to my hotel room. On the way back to the hotel, we dropped off Rafeek.

When the officer had fallen asleep in the back of the van, Rafeek took the opportunity to whisper a few instructions to me. He said to contact Zahid as soon as I got back.

"We are getting you out of here," he said.

I knew I had to operate with extreme discretion. If I somehow slipped up, I would jeopardize losing the tenuous upper hand I had managed to garner over the last few hours.

Back at my hotel, I already had some new clothes and toys that I had brought for Mati ahead of time. I had a beautiful hotel room, location carefully chosen in the diplomatic area of Dhaka. We were just a few short minutes away from the US Embassy.

While we worked things out, we had things handled.

I set Mati in a bubble bath. When he was contentedly playing with his toys, I took a moment to reach out separately to Zahid and Hans. I told them the news of our situation.

They said that we likely had only forty-eight hours to make our move. Our first step would be to get an emergency passport for Mati at the United States Embassy.

I had already completed the application. All I needed now was to get a valid photo of him, which I could pick up on the way to the embassy. Once we had that picture, Zahid and his assistant, Mashud, could make arrangements to get the necessary exit visa.

Zahid and I became nervous as we developed our plan. We knew that the hotel room phones could be easily tapped with listening devices, making them useless for our purposes. Khadijah's family had my cell phone numbers, so tracking my calls there would be exceptionally easy. We had to be careful and create new patterns of communication to work from.

We used Skype and a WhatsApp connection to pass messages back and forth. As far as we knew, these were still secure channels.

We continued to give off an appearance of normalcy. The following morning, I worked on the process of extending my visa. I kept up the illusion I was seeking long-term housing.

Zahid assured me that he was working on getting an exit visa. He was looking for any means of getting Mati safely out of the country. We carefully talked over the next steps.

Clearly, the situation was becoming delicate on Zahid's end as well. He was under extreme duress.

I arranged for an emergency meeting at the United States Embassy for the first thing in the morning; I planned on getting Mati's passport photo along the way.

Sharon Weber had been assigned to my case. She had become quite familiar with our situation. I pleaded with Sharon and her team for political asylum. I told her that my situation had turned bleak. I was tired of the constant bribes. I was desperate for my life, increasingly frightened by the threat of being assassinated.

A few times, I demanded that the State Department rescue Mati and me from the country by any means they could, as soon as possible. I argued that I needed political asylum in order to feel safe in a country that had rapidly turned from simply foreign to an outwardly hostile land. My life was on the line. To me, nothing in the terms of possibilities was off the table.

Maybe Sharon saw our situation the same way as well. What became clear, though, was that she could not meet my demands. Sharon pulled what strings she could, but a single solution through the American embassy was ultimately not in the cards for Mati and me.

All they could do, in the end, was give us an emergency passport and some sage advice.

"Whatever you do, Tyler," she said, "don't get caught."

By the look in her eyes, she was dead serious. I was out on a limb, on my own in a precarious state of limbo. My nation could do nothing more for me.

Mati and I walked out of that embassy meeting on a hot, humid afternoon. Our hopes had been deflated. We had been worn down to the nub, and now our options were winnowing with every passing hour.

We found ourselves on the muddled Dhaka streets with no driver and no phone. All I had was my son clinging to me, a briefcase with his emergency passport, and enough money to get us back to the hotel. Up to this point, I had rarely felt so alone in our struggle.

Eventually, we flagged down a rickshaw driver with an empty cart. We told him the name of the hotel where we were staying, but he didn't know where it was. Rather than wait and take a chance on another, we jumped on and did our best to navigate the way back home.

The driver carried us around and around the cramped streets. We were aimless. The dizzy route felt oddly familiar. We were without anchor, guessing around every turn where to go next. The route we took was much like the one Mati and I had taken together to become a family again.

We eventually arrived back at our hotel, albeit later than I had hoped. I paid and thanked the driver for his service and then scanned the faces around the doors. I didn't see anyone suspicious. Perhaps this was one of the rare moments that Mati and I were alone.

When I got back to the room, I had an urgent message from Zahid. As Mati curled up and napped on the bed, I called Zahid.

Zahid greeted my return call with excitement. While I was having my disappointing meeting with Sharon Weber, he had managed to pull some strings with higher-ups in the local government. I became ecstatic when he reported that he had the opportunity, with only a few executed documents, to get an exit visa in place for Mati.

"What's the next move then?" I asked.

Zahid said he was sending someone to the hotel immediately. A short while later Zahid's assistant, Mashud, arrived to get our signatures on the pertinent documents.

As quickly as his assistant came, he hurried away with only a few encouraging words. Once that paperwork was in place, we could make the bold move we had prepared for.

I let Mati sleep on the bed as I waited by the phone. In those quiet moments, I gathered whatever strength I had left for whatever would come next.

An hour after Mashud left my room with the documents in hand, Mati and I stepped out of the front doors of our hotel. I had a small pack loaded with a few necessities slung over one shoulder, and my son clinging happily to the other.

We appeared to be casual. We were dressed in light summer clothes, headed out toward no apparent destination.

Our luggage remained stowed back in our room. Anyone who might be checking up on our whereabouts would find all of my clothes still folded in the bureau drawers.

As we passed by the front lobby desk, I smiled and waved to the clerk on duty but did not check out of the room.

Everything we did gave the appearance that we would be coming back soon.

A taxi was waiting for us outside of the hotel. Mashud waited inside. He had the signed exit visa folded in what looked like an official envelope. He also had two plane tickets to Chittagong for Mati and me.

Anyone watching us from afar, checking up on our actions, would have assumed Mati and I were either going back to the embassy for another meeting or merely going to spend the day out in the city.

The Dhaka streets were jammed. That day everything had ground to a near standstill. I had never seen anything like it before in all my life.

All of the surface roads had been consumed by a general protest. Traffic was merciless. We waited through multiple changes of street lights. Car horns blared from all directions. People shouted and banged on our windows as we eased through crowds of street people, flooding the narrow thoroughfares in the neighborhood surrounding the hotel.

The driver turned back and apologized for our slow pace. I waved him off, no problem. Slow traffic did not matter. I saw the protests more as synergistic to what we were up to.

The more muddled and unpredictable our route could be right now, the better for executing our plan.

Mashud told the driver to take Mati and me to the domestic airport, which ended up being only a short distance from where our hotel was located. After navigating the chaotic streets, we pulled up to the departure terminal and prepared to board the first leg of our eventual escape.

I shook Mashud's hand and thanked him for everything. He wished me well and told me that Zahid would be waiting for us when we got to Chittagong.

We didn't think the domestic airport would be on anyone's radar. Chittagong had a smaller, more discreet international airport. That would be where we'd take off to freedom.

I smiled as we walked into the terminal. Mati did too. Acting in a friendly, natural way was our only defense against uncertainty.

To my relief, we passed through every checkpoint. Without issue, we casually walked up to our departure gate, boarded our cramped commuter plane, and took our seats beside one another. Moments later, we lifted off the runway to Chittagong.

The comfortable hum of a plane in flight took over our senses. Finally, we were in the air.

Mati and I breathed an enormous sigh of relief as Dhaka disappeared below us. We allowed ourselves a few moments to celebrate, but just a little bit. We had finally escaped our persecutors and the city that had kept us captive, but this was only the first leg. During that short forty-five-minute flight, the details of how our next move would play out crept into my thoughts. This victory had been a small one, but our next move would prove to be the most harrowing yet.

Welcoming faces awaited Mati and me in Chittagong. Zahid picked us up from the airport and we embraced like brothers reunited. Mati waited beside me for his introduction.

When the two finally met, Zahid walked us over to a nearby café and bought him an ice cream. Mati was delighted. Zahid was there with two of his best friends who, for the first time were given a chance to meet Mati, the center of this bitter custody fight. They took their turns, happily introducing themselves to him and congratulating me on getting this far. Mati was ecstatic to be out of Dhaka, and he remained the center of attention of the cheery group as night fell on Chittagong.

A great weight lifted off my shoulders as I watched Mati interact with Zahid and his friends. This was his first chance to act like a normal kid in a long time. I saw many of those aspects of his personality that I could only imagine before. My son possessed a silly sense of humor and a warm, kind way with people.

Mati was brave. But by now, I had already been aware that Mati was full of courage beyond his tender years. He'd had to be a brave child. If he were anything else, we would not have gotten this far already.

When we were alone, Zahid and I were able to speak more frankly. He placed a reassuring hand on my shoulder and offered his congratulations again. But it was time to get serious.

CHAPTER 8

• • •

WHEN I REFLECT ON WHAT my son and I went through to be together again, I never entertained the thought that it might be too dangerous. I never entertained the idea that Mati and I ventured too close to the edge. We had the love of a father and a son protecting us. I believe that. Now I do.

That does not mean I was not scared, though. What came after our arrival in Chittagong was one of the most frightening, hair-raising experiences of my life. If anything went wrong, if we were caught now, we would be hard pressed to gather the strength to go at it again. Of all the many times that I told myself or some other member of my team that we absolutely had to get this next step right, this was the time I meant it. After today, there would be no do overs.

Mati and I had escaped Dhaka but only to a place farther south in Bangladesh. Everyone knew that Chittagong was merely a stopover. We were nowhere near home yet. In order for us to get back home, we still had to pass through the rigors of international customs.

We had to leave the country, and in order to do that, we had to have all our paperwork in perfect working order. By now, everyone was probably aware that we were no longer staying in our hotel. They would be looking everywhere high and low for us. For us to escape back to the safety of the US and Florida, we had to be sure to evade any of Khadijah's family operatives along the way. They would almost certainly be checking airports, but which one?

Did they know we had connections in Chittagong? I wondered. I could not be certain that our position here was entirely secure. I did not fear for Mati's life. What I felt was a great fear for our life together. Khadijah's family had no reservations about hiring hit men and thugs. They most certainly would stop at nothing now.

I had hardly slept the night before, partly out of fear and anticipation. We were not going outside the law, I reminded myself. We were challenging the law to work in our favor. There was a slight difference, and it is one that I comforted myself in understanding.

There was nothing left for Hans, Zahid, Rafeek, or me to do in Bangladesh. We had exhausted ourselves getting what we needed, and now it was our time to enact the endgame. There was precious little left for any of us to say. Everything was out in the open; nothing remained for us to plan.

Night had already fallen for our anticipated red-eye flight. Like many of the other passengers leaving Shah Amanat International Airport that evening, Mati and I got out of the car. I slung our bag over my shoulder and stretched. Zahid got out also, and we shared a few embraces and said tearful good-byes.

Mati got his hug in and bounced happily while Zahid and I went over our last check. He was optimistic everything would work. Just in case, though, he would not be far from the airport until we were off the ground. Zahid said that he would be sitting outside, watching departing planes from a café, waiting for word on our safe passage through immigration.

As far as we could see, once we were through that critical checkpoint, all of our hard work and scrabbled-together documents would have proven effective. Beside a customary security check for bombs and weapons, we would be home free.

"Once you're through immigration, Tyler," Zahid said, "there should be Wi-Fi connectivity up to the gate."

"What happens if . . . ?"

Zahid assured me. "I don't think they have any means to arrest you," he said. "The worst thing that happens is I will come back for the two of you."

"OK," I replied. We were this far already. The worst possible thing I could think of was having to pick up and start over.

"When you and Mati are finally safe and secure," he said, "you have to let me know."

We embraced again. I had never felt so much brotherly kinship with another man like I did with Zahid. When we let go, he shot me his characteristically optimistic smile.

His expression had a sense of finality. Indeed there was nothing left for us to say.

I put my hand on Mati's shoulder, turned toward the dim light of the departing airline desks, and took a deep breath.

"Come on," I said. "Let's go."

As we entered the airport, we passed a couple of security guards. Mati was bubbling over with excitement. I tried my best to remain calm, in spite of my rapidly accelerating heart rate.

The airport was dingy. I had been in a few crude airports in back-water towns around the world, but this was one of the worst. I hid my discomfort as best I could and navigated Mati and me toward the appropriate line.

While we slowly approached the ticketing desk of our airline, Mati was goofing around. He was bursting with energy. I did my best to keep Mati in check. I did not want to draw any unnecessary attention to us, but it was becoming increasingly difficult to dampen his joy.

In Mati's mind, he was on his way home. I encouraged his optimism about this. I didn't want to do anything that might throw fear his way, but I knew that until we were through immigration, there was still an outside chance that we could be held up or apprehended.

If that happened, Zahid had his Plan B in place, but we would have lost our edge. We had tonight and an airline escape to work with the element of surprise. Tomorrow, our plan would be revealed and Khadijah's family would know.

We were booked onto a late flight on Biman Bangladesh Airlines. Biman is a fairly common local carrier that ran flights all over Asia. Our first leg was going from Chittagong to Dubai on the last Biman flight. I knew nothing specific about the airline, aside from the fact that when the clerk at the desk greeted us and asked me how I was, I was to smile and, once again, act natural. This would be the first gatekeeper.

I gave him my name and identification. I leaned on the counter and played with Mati while I waited for our tickets.

Immediately, however, we experienced a few complications. He checked my name and ID over and over against his records and eventually had to call in his supervisor for help. They commiserated while Mati played with his toys on the filthy airport floor.

What could possibly be going on? I thought as their brows furrowed between polite nods. I went through every possible nightmare scenario until I was exhausted.

Not wanting to raise a fuss, though, I smiled even brighter. I asked casually to see if there was a problem I could remedy. Minutes ticked away. They insisted the problem was no big deal, but still, every pause brought me a heightened sense of anxiety.

After a couple of minutes, Mati and I got our tickets. I picked my son up off the floor, said thank you, and walked out of ticketing with my heart pounding in my chest.

We walked down the hallway, past other passengers and airport officials. We moved past the pale light from the storefronts still open for business at this late hour.

Act naturally. Do not draw any attention. These were the thoughts that raced through my mind in rapid succession as we moved toward the departure terminal. I assured myself that Mati and I were nothing but a cute little pair, a father and his son on their way to an adventure.

We arrived at an escalator and staircase leading up to another level. All of the signs pointing up indicated that the immigration checkpoint would be up above.

Other people streamed past us as I stopped for a moment. I gathered Mati in my arms and made sure the backpack was secure. Then I stepped onto the first step.

Here we go, I thought.

Days ago, back in Dhaka, when the escorting police officer had momentarily fallen asleep on the dismal car ride from court back to our hotel, Rafeek had leaned over and assured me. "We're going to get you out. Don't worry, Tyler," he had said, secretively. "You two get back to the hotel and make contact with Zahid."

Zahid had his Plan A. And his Plan A was in full motion right now.

Zahid had a Plan B in his pocket as well. If for some reason Mati and I could not get through airport immigration for our escape by plane, we would try to go overland. It was Zahid's idea that we would drive from Chittagong, through the mountains, and into Burma. This would be an arduous route. We would take a car on a thirty-hour drive, over 1,200 dangerous kilometers where we would bargain our way to safety. It was a risky move, but I was assured that it was no less probable than Plan A.

However I tried to calm and assure myself, this was the possibility that was staring Mati and I in the face as we arrived at the top of the escalator and approached the immigration checkpoint. *Get through now*, I thought, *or be forced to pull back, turn around, and get in a car, only to face the whole awful and uncertain ordeal again.*

I didn't dare say any of this to Mati. He didn't need to know everything that was on the line for us. This would be my private angst, and as I looked around for where the line for immigration began, I took a series of deep, soothing breaths and did my best to suppress my anxiety further down into my stomach.

Keep calm, Tyler. Keep calm. All the two of you are is a father and son on an adventure.

When you are smuggling your child out of a foreign country under the kind of duress Mati and I were, even a five-minute delay can feel like an eternity. It's easy to laugh about all of it now in hindsight, but in that moment, the details and circumstances felt as strange and painful as I could imagine.

As Mati and I approached the immigration checkpoint on our way to the terminal, my heart was pounding against my rib cage. My stress-laden breaths became short; a few times I even forgot to breathe. I scanned the scene as we took our spot in line. People were coming off the escalator. They passed by one and two at a time. The security guards stood stoically, backs to the wall. I was the only white person I could see on this end of the airport. With Mati on my arm, I was almost certain we were making the kind of spectacle that would arouse suspicion.

"Come on, buddy," I said as we stepped to the back of the line.

The person in front of us glanced back and shot Mati a smile.

Happily, Mati stayed by my side. Heading off any chance at him becoming restless and drawing attention, I took a few of his toys out of my bag and arranged them on the floor for him to play with.

I maintained as much cool as I possibly could. I was careful not to give off any signals of what was by now overwhelming stress and aggravation.

The immigration official we would interact with seemed at first glance like a normal guy. I carefully watched the way he looked at the other people, how he examined their documents and passed them back with nary a second glance. I saw nothing notable in his demeanor or the cut of his simple uniform. In my worst nightmare, he would be a hard type, maybe someone higher up in the ranks with a grudge, but in reality, he appeared to be just like anyone else.

Mati played with his toys on the floor. With each passing passenger, we moved a few steps forward, and he would happily pick up and move his playthings, continuing at our next stop.

When our time finally came at the head of the line, I gathered up his toys and stuffed them in my bag before taking him in my arms.

I greeted the official. He shot a quick smile back.

"Your passports, please," he said, showing not a trace of emotion whatsoever.

I replied flatly. "OK."

Without hesitation, I pulled our two documents out of the front flap of my bag. My passport was old and worn out after years of use; Mati's was brand new, however, the edges and pages still crisp.

The official took them both in his hands. He looked at mine first and set it aside rather quickly. I breathed a welcome sigh of relief. We were halfway through.

The official's brow furrowed deeply, though, as he looked over Mati's passport. Even though he was a child and by virtue of his age, odds were he was on his first international flight, the fact that he had been handed a brand-new document must have drawn some attention.

I tried to pass off his second look as no big deal, but he could not be swayed. The official set Mati's passport aside near mine and asked coldly:

"Can I see your exit documentation?"

My heart leapt. I obliged him with a nod. *Stay confident*, I thought as I again reached into the backpack slung over my shoulder and pulled the documentation out for him to review.

"Here you are," I said.

The stamped exit visa was still in the crisp, fancy envelope that it had been delivered to me in earlier that day. My decision to keep it there had been a calculation with this moment in mind. I wanted to leave the good impression that everything was above board.

As the official opened up the envelope and pulled out the visa, he once again furrowed his brow. With pursed lips he disarmed us with a series of discerning looks.

Did he see that cute couple, father and son, on an adventure that I had envisioned for Mati and me? Or did he see something else? Did he see two desperate people on the run? Our eyes showed the wear of travel and obvious exhaustion. Had he caught onto us?

After an agonizing moment under scrutiny, the official gathered up all of our documents. He looked at Mati and looked at me with an officious nod.

"Wait here a moment, please," he said, then without another word, he vanished into the little office that stood adjacent to his post and closed the door.

I clutched Mati tight. Mati clutched me back. He, too, seemed to sense that we had arrived at a crucial point in our escape plan.

Zahid's words echoed back in my mind. They likely did not have enough cause to arrest us. Even though I felt somewhat encouraged by his giving that impression, the delay was torturous. I was done with turning around and starting over. I wanted nothing to do with taking the mountain road to Burma.

I looked back over my shoulder. The immigration line had filled up with other prospective passengers. They mostly seemed bored while waiting for their turn.

The security guards back at the top of the stairs had not moved from their posts since we passed. So far, my best guess was that we had not drawn any more attention than normal.

Inside the office, the immigration official was taking his time. Although I could not tell exactly what he was doing with our passports and visas, I knew he was looking the documents over with a careful eye. He rubbed his chin. He moved to another position and went through some motions before I saw the back-and-forth lights of a photocopier illuminate his chin.

What is he doing? I thought. This could not be a good sign.

Once he had his copies made, the immigration official pushed back through the door and returned to his post. I braced for the worst, but for an awful, sickening second, he did not speak.

I clutched Mati even tighter as he laid our documents on the counter between us.

"Safe travel," he said.

I didn't respond as the official motioned to the next person in line. Then I realized we were through. I said a quick thanks and clumsily took up our paperwork.

In total, the immigration process took no more than twenty minutes; in my mind, though, it felt more like an hour. Once we were through the checkpoint and I could see the clerk move on to grilling his next person, I whisked Mati away in my arms and moved on as fast as I could.

As the immigration checkpoint slowly faded into the background, I felt my stress level ease up some. Tension went out of my limbs. I began to breathe a little easier.

Mati and I had gotten through the most dangerous choke point so far, but I was well aware that we were not home free yet. Until our wheels were off the ground and we were in the air away from this awful place, there was still an outside chance that we would be apprehended.

I clutched my son's hand as we moved slowly down the hallway toward the snaking line for TSA's security check. Cops prowled the area, lazy eyes on the comings and goings. I watched as one by one, passengers set their bags on conveyor belts and passed through full-body scanners under the watchful eye of uniformed security. The scene was a familiar one I had been through a hundred times, but the peculiar strain of the moment left me feeling ill at ease.

I could sense Mati was excited, though. The bounce in his step told me he felt our escape was imminent. We had to strike a balance, and I did my best to temper his childish exuberance.

"Almost, OK?" I said.

Mati nodded. He was cool and assumed a mature posture as we moved on.

"We still have to keep calm until we get on the plane."

My eyes never stopped scanning the scene as we crept forward in line. The TSA security check proved to be time consuming but ultimately uneventful. My shoes went off. Our bag passed through the customary scanner, and our bodies were patted down, but all Mati and I got from the officials were a couple of short smiles and the urge to take our things and move on.

This might really happen, I thought excitedly, gathering our things and hurrying away from security. A few paces down the hallway, I saw the sign for our departure gate and recognized how little stood in the way of our family's reunion.

I stopped short of our departure gate. I gave Mati some toys and he happily resumed his play while I set about logging into the Wi-Fi.

I had to tell Zahid that we had made it.

Zahid burst out excitedly as I told him where I was standing. I heard a few rowdy cheers go up, followed by the clinking of celebratory beers as word of our safe passage spread around their bar table. They gave no more words of caution, only happy bursts of revelry.

Reality began to sink in. This might happen.

Zahid told me that he and his men would stay where they were until they saw our plane was in the air, something they could see from the bar where they had camped out for the evening. Their tone would transform from anticipatory to celebratory.

For what must have been the hundredth time over the last few weeks, I said thank you to Zahid for all he had done for my family. My gratitude never felt excessive. Given the friendship Zahid and I had, I could feel nothing but sincere gratitude.

As we staggered into the gate of the Biman Bangladeshi flight that serviced a large swath of southern Asia, it occurred to me in what capacity that service was used.

The waiting passengers were mostly poor and destitute-looking Bengalis. Our red-eye flight was a migrant worker shuttle, used for shipping what appeared to be cheap manual labor to the exploding wealth center of Dubai. Bangladesh was still a third-world country, and the huddled masses waiting for their flight was a stark reminder of what Mati would be leaving.

The relatively desperate company we would keep while we were in the air to Dubai proved to be no deterrence, though. I watched as the clock slowly ticked down to departure. Mati and I did our best to contain the enthusiasm we shared. We were another step closer to safety, patiently waiting for our seat row to be called for boarding.

When we finally heard ours called out, we lined up and politely passed through the usual routine of handing over boarding passes and exchanging niceties. Neither of us bothered to look back over our shoulders and say good-bye as the airport vanished down the ramp.

I was never coming back. I was certain Mati felt the same way.

Our airplane could be described as nothing short of disgusting. As Mati and I settled into our ragged, dirty seats, I got up to use the bathroom. I found the facilities were cramped. They had apparently not been serviced in years. As I got my bearings, I noticed cockroaches crawling on the floor around the toilet and up the sides of the battered vanity.

I did not bother to wash my hands. I decided to keep the clean clothes I had brought along to change into in our carry-on bag. As I returned to our seat, I told Mati that we would hold tight and freshen up when we were on the ground at our destination. He didn't seem to mind.

Mati and I buckled our safety belts on command. It was the last minute, but I still watched every passing movement for anything suspicious.

Over the intercom, someone announced that the cabin door had been closed in preparation for takeoff. The jovial pilots settled into the cockpit. They said a few words to the flight attendants and then closed the doors behind them.

An air of anticipation raced through the plane. No one could have been more excited than Mati and me. We heard the engines outside warm up. Another series of flight announcements were made and I watched as the other attendants got into position for takeoff.

I held Mati's hand as the cabin went dark. *Here we go!*

The plane backed away from the terminal. Mati closed his eyes, but a coy smile remained on his face throughout as we pulled back. The building disappeared outside the windows.

Then all I could see was darkness and the flashing lights of the runway. I felt Mati's little hand tense a bit as the plane straightened out and we began to taxi toward take off.

Then the plane lurched suddenly forward. The ancient aircraft made a few awkward, clattering sounds as the cabin lights dimmed further and we gathered speed.

A panicked thought raced through my addled mind. With bathrooms as awful as those, what if the plane itself was in similar disrepair?

Then I closed my eyes, too, and took a deep breath. Outside, the wings rattled. My seat creaked under the strain of gathering speed. Normally these sounds would arouse an air of caution, even fear. Not today, though. *We're home free*, I thought. I held Mati's hands even tighter.

Then I felt the plane lift off the ground. First, the nose lifted upward toward the sky and the rest of the plane followed. The flashing runway lights vanished underneath us.

I breathed a sigh, perhaps the deepest, most relieved sigh I had ever emitted. We were finally airborne. There was nothing anyone could do to tear Mati and me apart anymore.

But Mati's excitement for the moment could not be contained. As our steep incline gradually leveled off toward cruising altitude, we took out my phone and snapped a few pictures to mark the moment. We celebrated as the plane arced west over India, and Bangladesh disappeared under the plane. We embraced fully, in the way that only free people can.

Mati and I were going to be father and son after all.

When the flight attendants began passing through the cabin a few moments later with carts loaded with drinks and food, Mati and I politely refused their offer of service. Both of us were hungry and thirsty, but somehow the thoughts of cockroaches in the bathroom gave me pause. We decided it would be better to wait until we were on the ground in Dubai.

Done with celebrating, exhausted, and spent from our narrow escape, Mati yawned. He crawled onto my body and curled into my arms, where he dozed off.

I stroked his greasy hair. I brushed his slackened cheek with my finger as his breath slowed and he began to snore. He was pale. At first glance, he did not look healthy.

What mattered most in that moment was happiness and what came next for him. For the first time in a long time, Mati was happy and at ease, and that would serve as our new start.

I smiled. Then I promptly felt myself falling asleep too.

This was the way Mati and I spent the remainder of the five-and-a-half-hour flight to Dubai, asleep in each other's arms. One of my last fleeting thoughts was that somewhere down on the ground, Zahid and his friends were celebrating.

Throughout the flight I roused from my slumber a few times. I stirred infrequently to the sounds of an aircraft in flight or someone brushing past us on the aisle, nudging against my leg with the drink cart. Mati would squirm or fidget and my eyes would open, only to loll peacefully back to sleep without concern. I was no longer the bundle of nerves I had been throughout the last few weeks in Bangladesh; I felt no threat of anyone sneaking up to grab us out of our peaceful sleep. Each time I stirred and felt my son's gentle breath on me, I was filled with a transcendent kind of happiness. It had been a long time since I'd known this kind of peace.

The pilot announced that we were into our gradual descent toward the airport. Mati and I awoke and shook off the cobwebs of a fitful sleep. When we eventually touched the ground in Dubai, it was four thirty in the morning. Mati and I rose to our feet and quietly filed out.

The normally bustling airport hub was sparsely populated at this early hour. The droves of Bengali workers on our flight filed out and vanished toward their ground transportation.

Mati was wide-eyed and quiet as we moved out into the airport. Few other people surrounded us. The early shift of workers was just coming on. A few other weary red-eye passengers dragged their lethargic bodies off of an arriving flight. Otherwise, we felt like we had the whole place to ourselves.

Mati and I still had a nearly four-hour layover in front of us. As we gathered our bearings in the massive, ultramodern complex, I became acutely aware of how filthy we were.

Pressed at every juncture either for time or discretion, neither one of us had had the opportunity to wash up in nearly a day. We were both still wearing the same dirty clothes we had worn when we escaped from our Dhaka hotel thirty-six stress-filled hours ago. We were ripe and needed to freshen up. A shower sounded terrific, but that unfortunately was not an option.

Although Mati and I were both also ravenously hungry, we decided it would be best to first change out of the clothes we had on into something clean. I saw the universal sign for a men's bathroom up ahead. "Come on," I said, and hand in hand, we dashed down the empty hall.

The bathroom was brightly lit and appeared as though it had recently been remodeled. The cleanliness and order was suddenly comforting.

Finding myself out of the chaos of Bangladesh, back in the realm of modern comforts like functional bathrooms made me feel even closer to home. I scanned under the stalls to see if we were alone. I saw no one else.

"Let's get your clothes off," I said.

I set Mati up on the counter. He stuck his hands high up in the air. I gently stripped off his shirt and pants and threw them aside in a heap. He giggled. Although I could tell that he was physically drained, he bounced a little, eager to make this dressing ritual a game. When he was down to his underwear, he proudly rubbed his skinny chest and smiled.

I ran the faucet until the stream under my fingers warmed. I waited till the water was just right before I rinsed him off. I lathered up my hands with soap and, using a balled-up paper towel, I gently gave him a sponge bath. His flesh washed clean. He began to smell fresh again.

Mati thrilled as the warm water cascaded. He livened up as layers of filth and sweat washed away from his arms, chest, and belly. He placed his little hands on my shoulders as his feet dangled over the edge and I reached around, applying the same care to his back and legs.

As I pulled my shirt off to do the same, Mati finally broke our silence. "You know something, Daddy?" he said.

"What?" I replied, mind still in the sponge bath mode.

"I love my sister and I love my mommy too," he explained. "But I love you more than anything else, and I just want to be with my daddy from now on."

My chest warmed as I lowered to one knee and brought my eyes into intimate contact with his. Mati was absolutely sincere. It was written in his tender gaze. I couldn't help but smile. This little boy who had experienced more of the base ugliness in people at such an impressionable age than most people will endure in a lifetime was opening for a heart-to-heart.

"If that's what you want, buddy," I said, uncertain whether or not I should try and mask how choked up with emotion I was. "Then that's all I want too."

We embraced. We held each other tightly, skin to skin, never wanting to let go.

"OK," he said, satisfied.

Each embrace in this new place of freedom felt deeper, but as badly as I wanted to linger there in that heartfelt, affirming place forever, the moment eventually passed, although something told me it was what now defined us. Mati and I were a father and son, whole and complete.

Mati helped me wash up. He took his turn with soap and a fresh set of balled-up paper towels, scrubbing my back, making monkey sounds as he washed the stink from under my arms. His cute, childish giggles turned into little bursts of laughter as we splashed around in the bathroom sink. If someone else had come through the bathroom in those moments, I am not sure if we would have noticed his or her presence.

When we were finally done and dressed, we took all of our old clothes and wrapped them up in a smelly ball. I let Mati run with them and throw them in the trash as we walked out. Those clothes were remnants of the old world. A new world was what awaited us.

Onto our next need, Mati and I hurried out of the bathroom, following the signs to the food court to see what was open for us to choose from. By now both of us were starving and in desperate need of a decent meal to tide us over.

The airport was already much busier, although it was still early in the morning. Men from all over the world wearing business suits, and families on their way to a vacation, streamed past us as we looked over the restaurants.

Our body clocks had been thrown wildly off. The hour on the clock seemed irrelevant in choosing what to eat. Was this a late dinner or an early breakfast, I wasn't quite sure.

"What do you want?" I asked.

Mati grinned. Our best choice seemed quite clear.

"How about an ice cream?" he suggested.

An ice cream cone, the universal salve for a tired and stressed-out child who has just endured a once-in-a-lifetime day, at the end of an epic ordeal that he would surely tell people about for many years to come. I shrugged and agreed.

"OK, buddy," I said. "If that's what you want, you got it."

Mati and I lined up. We ordered mountainous scoops of ice cream and spoons full of crumbled toppings. For a moment, I entertained thoughts about good parenting, only for the briefest moment, though, before I let it go. Whether or not this was a proper food choice seemed a debate better undertaken on another day. I encouraged Mati to get whatever he wanted, no holds barred. We had been through enough, and for now, we would throw caution to the wind. Lavishing my son with a morning treat was a luxury I had been denied for too long.

We got our ice cream and found a quiet place to sit down in the food court. Mati was thrilled with each spoonful. As other travelers ate their breakfast and drank tea inconspicuously around us, we pulled out my phone and posed for another series of pictures.

Mati stood up on his chair. He waved his arms wildly. I didn't care what we looked like to anyone passing by. Our silly shots of celebration had been well earned.

As I look back, Mati's expression in those pictures said so much. He was uninhibited. His laughter burst forth without caution. No one was telling him what to say and feel anymore, nor would anyone from this point forward.

Mati was breaking free and, like moments before in the bathroom, I wanted to linger in that carefree moment as long as I possibly could.

My expression in the pictures tells as much. I am in awe of him. I am taking his lead as he offers himself to the camera. I, too, am breaking free.

Around ten in the morning local time, Mati and I arrived at our departure gate. By now the airport was teeming with people and noise. My head was heavy with exhaustion, but I felt something else, a different pressure. I could tell that I was getting sick.

Mati yawned over and over. He could barely keep himself from falling asleep on his feet. As we took our seats, he settled down to play on the floor with his toys while I logged online and went directly to social media.

Word was already spreading through my community. Well wishes and congratulations were filtering in one at a time.

I uploaded the pictures we took in the food court and broadcast the details of our escape: *Mati and I about to get on an Emirates Flight. Next stop, New York and JFK*, I wrote.

CHAPTER 9

• • •

So much of our daring escape from Bangladesh was orchestrated from behind the scenes.

Zahid and I, and the rest of my team, devised our own unique language in order to communicate important information out of sheer necessity. We talked through back channels. We waited for police officers to fall asleep in the back seat in order to pass along crucial messages. We jumped from one technology platform to skirt tapped phones and texts in an attempt to keep one step ahead of our dogged pursuers.

Nothing could ever be taken for granted. Every effort had to be given to maintaining an air of secrecy. As our ordeal in court proved, even communication about my case with our corrupt Supreme Court lawyers was taking a chance on exposure.

If word of our plans had gotten out in the wrong way, Mati and I could have been compromised. Danger lurked around every corner. Any leak could have led to our apprehension, my son's permanent sequester in Dhaka, and as I learned later on, my assassination at the hands of any one of the hit men waiting in the weeds. Consequently, everything took place on a need-to-know basis.

Until our plane lifted off the ground, my team ran on a razor's edge every minute of every day. As glamorous as those elements of espionage might sound, life lived in isolation tends to be a lonely place. No one can reach out to you because no one knows.

Back home in Naples, all of my friends and my family had, for the most part, been kept in the dark about what was going on in Dhaka. My parents received precious few communications regarding my status and whereabouts. My close friends received a few sporadic words here and there about my wellness, everything filtered down from Zahid. His hurried word was all anyone had to go on.

I also had another, more personal factor to consider in keeping my loved ones mostly in the dark. Beyond the obvious risk to our lives and our operation, we felt it would be best to keep the frightening details away from those who were helpless to come to our rescue. The way my team saw it, the less anyone knew about the bribes and hit men, the better, let alone the odds, which at many points along the way felt stacked against Mati and I ever getting home. I wanted to be honest with everyone, and for a while, what was honest wasn't pleasant.

Our ordeal was agonizing, especially when viewed from the other side of the world. As my family and I got slowly reacquainted and I filled in the details, I learned that those long weeks were filled with protracted silences, punctuated by moments of oblique uncertainty.

Zahid had reached out to my mother a few times. When he got through to her, his message was desperate, cloaked in mystery. He sent emails. He asked for her prayers to Allah. Once, Zahid asked that she try and make contact with anyone who might be able to help our plight. When my mother received that request, she called a State Department emissary assigned to Bangladesh. When they spoke, she was surprised to learn that he already knew my story. But what did that mean? My mother and father endured the same time in darkness.

When I broadcast my status update of Mati and I through Facebook, all of our previous discretion and pacts of silence went away in the single press of a button.

Send. And suddenly, everyone knew.

As we got on our plane in Dubai, my world was only hours away from waking up to the details of our fate.

• • •

Zahid watched the taillights of our plane as it slowly lifted off the runway in Chittagong. He breathed a deep sigh of relief, lit a cigarette, and downed the rest of his beer. His hands trembled, he was so exhilarated.

All around him, his friends, our allies, celebrated. They cheered and hugged one another as we vanished westward into the autumn night. Every one of them knew what our departure meant. They had all had a hand in accomplishing something special. They had successfully helped a father and his son, trapped halfway around the world, to get safely home again. They had not only saved two lives from an ugly fate; they had saved a family.

With tears still in his eyes, Zahid pulled his cell phone out of his pocket. He took a fresh beer and cigarette from the table and found a quiet place away from the noise. He had another phone call to make—to my parents back in Naples.

Zahid had my mother's phone number programmed, although they had never spoken to one another before. Throughout the ordeal, they had exchanged emails, but until the phone rang, interrupting my mother's real estate class, they hadn't heard one another's voices.

"Hello, Yvonne," Zahid said. "This is Zahid."

She replied, breath held tight: "Hello Zahid." His call could have meant anything.

It was a sunny October day in Naples, Florida, a few days short of Halloween. She put down her things and hurried out of the classroom with her phone clutched to her chest, looking for somewhere private that she could speak to him outside.

"OK, OK . . ."

"I want to tell you," Zahid said, "that you are going to get your son and grandson back very soon."

By now Zahid's voice was trembling with joy. The moment's pause was enough to build his anticipation. Sometimes the words you know you must say are the hardest to get out.

"When their wheels left the ground," he continued, filling in details, "it was the happiest moment of my life."

My mother clamored for words she could not quite find. In the end, she echoed the same sentiments that I had so many times.

"Thank you."

Two words that mean so much, but somehow cannot ever capture everything.

After they were done talking, my mother hung up the phone. Going back to her lecture seemed suddenly outside the realm of possibility. Instead, she wandered the lush garden paths around the building where her class was taking place. Everything seemed lighter, more beautiful.

The news was unbelievable. The few tears she shed while talking with Zahid released into an utter torrent of happiness. She was going to get her son and grandson back, and soon.

For weeks, my mother and father lived their day-to-day lives under a black cloud. They tried to go about things as though everything was normal, but they were not. With so much hanging in the balance, nothing could be normal. My mother kept herself going on those messages from Zahid. She had gotten a few emails from Hans along the way, too. It felt terrible, but my mother only received brief words from me even though I wanted desperately to keep them in the loop. Knowing how much they would worry about me, I chose silence. Another few weeks may have broken down their resolve, but now those clouds had lifted and nothing could ever bring them back again. The revelation was earth shattering.

My mother called my father to take her turn passing along the good news. Then she went back home and prepared for our homecoming.

That night, instead of lying around the house with phones on stand-by to answer in case of an emergency, my mother and father decided to go out. They got dressed up in fancy clothes and had dinner with a few close friends. It was not intended to be a celebratory dinner, but that's what it turned out to be. They knew that tomorrow everyone would finally be reunited.

For Zahid, once he'd finished all the cold, hard-earned beers and his friends had broken up for the evening, he decided it was time to go home as well. For a few days he had been away, too.

When his wife greeted him at the door, Zahid broke down into tears once again. All of the secrecy and scheming were done, and a space opened up, one filled by raw emotion.

Our escape was, as Zahid would confess later on, one of the greatest things he had ever been a part of. Yet, throughout the whole, long ordeal, Zahid had decided he would not tell his wife what he was up to.

Until he walked through the door, she had no idea about Mati and me. She had no idea her husband's life had been threatened by Khadijah's family. He had gone about his business and agonizing quietly. Our needed pact of secrecy had forced Zahid to keep everything bottled up inside.

But as he saw her again in that moment, he could not bear to keep those secrets inside any longer. Secrets can burn a hole in a marriage. They wear down honest men. And that's what Zahid was, an honest man who would now tell his wife why she found him weeping.

Zahid told his wife everything. He told her about Mati and me. He described our struggle with Khadijah and her powerfully influential family. He told her about smuggling us out of Dhaka, and our narrow escape through airport immigration and security.

Then he told her how it all ended, in a breathtaking conversation he'd had with my grateful mother only moments ago.

• • •

After our lengthy, four-hour layover in Dubai, Mati and I boarded our connecting flight. We were headed to John F. Kennedy airport in New York City. Although we were still both excited, our bodies had rapidly arrived at a point far beyond exhaustion. Another thirteen hours in the air battered our delirious minds even further. At least conditions on this plane were clean enough that we felt safe accepting offers of food and drink, and even using the bathroom.

When we arrived in New York, the idea that we were hitting ground in the United States did not come with the same sense of celebration. We were already free. Now all we wanted to be was home, and in order to reach our end destination, we still had one more flight to take.

By now, Mati and I were both sick. We had both picked up awful head colds from what was almost a full twenty-four hour trek crossing the globe by air. We had been in and out of airports and planes, exposure that would cripple even healthy, well-rested passengers, let alone those coming out on the other side of a month-long struggle filled with stress and anguish.

I booked whatever direct flight I could find that would get Mati and me from New York into the Miami area. Once we had our tickets in hand, I called my parents and told them when they could come pick us up at the airport in Miami.

When we got on the plane, we must have looked terrible. I was haggard. Mati was still in good spirits, but he was worn down.

"One more time, buddy," I said, doing my best to encourage him.

After four hours in the air that seemed somehow like the longest leg of them all, we landed on the ground in Miami. We passed out of security, into the open air where we found my eager parents.

Mati ran blissfully into their open arms. Although his cold was getting worse with every passing hour, he was outwardly exuberant to see them. I watched as they came together as one; my parents swallowed him up joyfully, covering his sweaty face with a bushel of kisses. They didn't care that he was sick. He was whole and back in their arms again.

Although I was equally happy to see them, I felt as though each embrace was leading me closer to a total physical collapse. When we hugged, it felt like they were holding me up. Throughout this ordeal, I had been leaning on others for support. This was the best feeling of all.

My parents set us up in their car, and we drove for two hours, through the Everglades back home to Naples.

We arrived on the Gulf Coast in the middle of the night. I can honestly say I have never been so happy to see Naples in all of my life. Although only a month had passed since I'd left, my house felt strange. It was as though a lifetime had passed. I was a different person now. We were.

We were back where we belonged. Finally.

Somewhere in that journey home, I promised Mati that he would never, ever have to leave the United States again, unless he absolutely wanted to. He was happy to hear it.

My pledge did not seem unreasonable when I considered that at the time of our escape, Mati was five years old and he had already traveled more than most people ever do.

Mati and I arrived home on Halloween, a night I will never be able to look at quite the same way again.

Like a wildfire, word of our escape spread throughout my community. Those tenuously held walls had fallen down completely.

Not long after we were safely in the air, Hans received the good news of our successful passage through immigration. Rafeek learned by way of Zahid that we had made it through as well. They both celebrated in their own way and sent their well wishes to my family.

Texts came through on my phone. Celebratory messages arrived via email. By the time we had gotten to New York, my Facebook post with our pictures had dozens of responses.

There was still the matter of how this revelation would shake out with Khadijah, however.

Between airport checkpoints at immigration and security in Chittagong, before we boarded our plane, I had left Khadijah a few messages. What I conveyed to her had been carefully crafted. I thought out every word. Although by that point I was fairly certain that Mati and I were for the most part in the clear, I figured it would not hurt our cause to run a little more interference her way.

So far everything had been about proper timing, and for all I knew, Khadijah's family could have had one of their henchmen ready to spring on us at our departure gate.

Our ordeal had taught my team to prepare for, and even expect, the element of surprise.

I connected and told Khadijah that everything was going well. I said that we had just sat down to eat a late dinner. I told her that after Mati and I were done eating, it would be into the bath and then time for bed. I wanted to assure her that we were following the prescribed routine.

I was still not sure what Khadijah was aware of. If her family had caught on to any part of what Mati and I were up to, I had been given no inclination so far. Hours passed, and by the time Mati and I stepped off that plane in the Dubai airport, what Khadijah knew or did not know about our whereabouts became quite clear.

From the sound of things, all hell had broken loose in Dhaka.

When I turned my phone back on to inform everyone that we had made it, I found a long list of messages waiting for me. A few were from my family. Others were from friends who knew the struggle I was embroiled in. I had received a happy message from anyone who had gotten the good news through Zahid, passing their best wishes along to Mati and me.

As I expected, more than a few of those waiting messages were from Khadijah. What she had to say did not matter anymore. I listened to them one after another with morbid curiosity. At first she came off as relatively calm, which was somewhat surprising to me as I gauged the increasing stress in her voice.

"Where is he?" she would ask. "Where have you and Mati gone?"

She calmly pleaded for answers using her best concerned voice. She was begging to know, like any other worried mother would, desperate to know what was going on with her son.

That calmly concerned tone soon took a dramatic change.

As the messages progressed, Khadijah became increasingly dark. She cursed and made every manner of threat. This woman who had walled off any of my attempts at communication with utter impunity for months on end, was now calling me repeatedly, one call after another. She had clearly found my phone number in her contacts.

"You cannot take him away from us, Tyler," she said in what I knew by now was a pale and meaningless threat. She hissed, and her voice escalated into screams. At times she was relentless, and I turned the phone away from my ear to let it all pass by.

"You and your family will all be in a lot of trouble if you actually think you're going to get away with this." Everything Khadijah said was delivered with menace.

But what could she actually do to back that up? Khadijah had been reduced to throwing out empty promises. She was making threats of harm that she could not possibly back up with anything more than her characteristic anger.

Only now the tables had abruptly turned. She could throw one of her fits, but no one needed to take them seriously anymore.

Somewhere during the course of our flight while we slept, Khadijah must have come to the realization that Mati and I were not just ducking our return to them in Dhaka. She had to have figured out that we had fled Bangladesh altogether. It dawned on her that we had ended up somewhere farther than her family's reach could possibly extend.

Then another even more curious shift in her tone occurred. Her belligerent stance turned abruptly around. Khadijah actually sounded diplomatic, something strange that I had never heard from her in all of our relationship.

"Very well, Tyler," she said at last. "You have won this. When can I see my son?"

In that moment, I could hear that Khadijah was a broken woman who had gotten precisely what she deserved. Someone had told her to give up. She was all alone.

Her voice had tears of sadness when she asked, "When can I talk to him?"

In spite of all my celebratory feelings, none of her anguish gave me any real sense of joy. I knew all too well the pain and isolation of an estranged parent. She was in my shoes now.

On the other hand, I could not quite bring myself to produce any empathy for her situation. That was a leap I could not make then and cannot make now. On all things regarding Khadijah, I had become comfortably numb.

The way I saw things, the road to our compromise had been laid out and generously explained to her, and at every turn, she had chosen not to take it. She had steadfastly refused. In our growing estrangement, Khadijah had sought something else. She wanted complete and total control of our child, a dangerous stance in the bitter throws of a lengthy custody struggle.

I had told her time and again that I would never let that happen, and she didn't hear me. She had chosen to ignore my resolve, which was ultimately her downfall.

For longer than a year by this point, Khadijah had deliberately flaunted any attempt to work out a mutually beneficial solution to our parenting agreement. None of the lawyers and mediators and court orders compelled her to the diplomacy she had now.

The road she chose was a bitter one filled with strife. She had gotten everyone in her family to back her, and instead of working things out, they geared up for an all-out conflict.

And in every conflict, without fail, someone has to lose.

That person was Khadijah. Her message was correct. I had definitely won. But there was an even better way of thinking of the outcome we had arrived at.

Mati had won.

Out of all this chaos and isolation, Mati had finally received a loving father, unflagging support in the form of my family, and now had a beautiful life in front of him.

That's the way I chose to think of it, even back then, in the sleepy terminal of the Dubai airport. Out all of this pain, Mati was the winner, a victory that was a team effort.

After hearing all of Khadijah's messages, I hung up the phone and put it away. I would not take the time to dignify them with a response. I had nothing left to say to her.

I took my son's hand in mine and we set about the task of getting a well-deserved, early morning ice cream.

• • •

Even after we were safely back, recovering at home in Naples, Khadijah's family continued going through the motions. Everything they did was for appearance. They tried to track Mati and me down through Bangladesh. They sent members of the Dhaka police to investigate our hotel. The officers went in and tore my room apart, searching for any evidence I may have left behind in our flight to safety. I wondered what they could possibly be looking for that could change anything. This realization filled me with a growing sense that her family must be reaching a collective sense of exhaustion from defending her antics. I'd left nothing incriminating behind for them to find. Even if they had found any of our papers, messages, or transcripts of our scheming, they would not have mattered. They could not compel us to return. I was, as Hans and I constantly established, on the right side of the law at every turn.

Still, for some reason, they persisted in grasping at straws. Anything to save face.

My luggage still sat where I'd left it, packed by the door of the hotel. All Khadijah's family got for their concerted efforts were some summer clothes and a few toiletries.

Later on, I made a few attempts to retrieve my luggage, but officials at the hotel told me that even they were not allowed access to it. The police would still not permit them. My luggage was part of an open investigation, they said. It was connected to an inquiry that would seemingly arrive at no end. At least no end that I cared about.

To this day, and to the best of my knowledge, that luggage, a curious part in our story, is still sitting in a room somewhere at that Dhaka hotel.

Let it go, I think. Like so many other things, it is merely a footnote in the whole story. Turns out, summer clothes and toiletries are a small price to pay for a son's happiness.

Even as Khadijah had shown a few glimmers of diplomacy with me in the interest of a relationship with her son, she was not through with her assault.

Not long after Mati and I had settled into a routine in Florida, Khadijah took to the offensive. This time she decided to take a few vicious stabs in the dark at members of my team.

She made calls and sent emails. She was throwing out volleys of displaced anger. She was really angry with me and perhaps with herself, but that didn't cool her rage.

At this point, everything seemed like a natural last gasp in the face of abject humiliation.

Although I had no idea how she had made some of those connections, when I got word of her outbursts, I cannot say I was surprised in the least.

She made contact with Rafeek, my attorney whom she knew from the trials. How she found Hans I don't quite know, but she threatened each of them without hesitation. She made promises of hellacious reprisal for what they had done to hurt her and defame her family.

Hans and Rafeek passed off the threats, disregarded them for exactly what they were. Although both men were professionally tied to Bangladesh, they knew these threats were desperate histrionics from a wounded person, grasps in the dark without much merit.

Khadijah's attack on Zahid turned out a little differently, though. When she called him up, she came across as vicious and hateful. She held nothing back. She threatened to harm both Zahid and his family.

"Sleep with one eye open," she told Zahid. She told him that her people were coming for him and they would get revenge for what they had done to her.

Zahid was not impressed by her threats. Instead of simply ignoring Khadijah, though, he decided to turn the tables. Although I never heard the conversation, in my imagination it was fierce.

After hearing her threats, Zahid fired back at her. He told Khadijah that she was indeed barking up the wrong tree. He told her he could crush her if he chose to.

"Don't you threaten me or my family, little girl, understand?" he said. "You do not know who you're messing with right now."

I can only imagine what her response might have been.

When Zahid and I spoke a few days after their altercation, we caught up on our lives before he launched into a detailed account of his entire conversation with Khadijah.

I was floored. I knew that Khadijah had some nerve, but this was something else. By the time she had gotten off the phone with Zahid, she had been put in her place.

"Is it over?" I asked.

"She won't be making any more threats to me or my family," he replied.

Khadijah had just learned the hard way what I had discovered from working with Zahid. He is not a man that you mess with. Zahid is not someone you want on your bad side. Again, I thanked him for all he had done.

Before we parted ways, Zahid offered me a few words of caution.

"Khadijah is not good, Tyler," he said. "You need to know that she is a very dangerous person. I would not allow her to get anywhere close to that son of yours."

CHAPTER 10

• • •

A COUPLE OF YEARS HAVE passed since Mati and I escaped Bangladesh. This is how I like to think of it, looking back.

I got my son back in my life. And Mati got his dad.

The way I try and look at life now, my son and I rescued one another. We were saved from a bleak future spent an ocean apart that neither of us would have been happy living.

Mati and I live together close to my family. We are always going in and out of one another's homes, supporting each other. My parents have become a regular part of his upbringing.

Our group of friends remains plentiful and close knit. Mati has made a lot of connections at school, and I have taken an active role in his education ever since he first enrolled. This is the paradise I long ago envisioned, providing for my family. I simply never knew that it would take such an ordeal to get here.

Each day that I am able, I rollerblade Mati to school in his "chariot," the bright orange jogging stroller he has had since he was little.

When Mati gets out for the day, I scoop him up in his chariot and rollerblade him over to the Naples Botanical Garden and the surrounding lakes to do his homework. This is one of the most beautiful gardens in the world, an ideal environment for learning. Mati is a sharp kid. He is curious about life, maybe because he has already had so many of its complexities revealed to him at such a tender age. Consequently, Mati asks a lot of questions. And in this way, he's a lot like his dad.

Like everything else regarding my ex-fiancée, the truth around Khadijah over the years comes to us in fleeting, uncertain glimpses. For my own sake, I don't care about what her next chapter might look like, except when it comes to answering Mati's curiosities.

Once Mati and I were gone, the war and the charade were abruptly over. She dropped out of my life, never to turn and look back.

When I think back on the way she must have felt when she learned that we got away, I feel conflict. I don't thrive on suffering. On one hand, I feel for any parent who loses a child. On the other hand, Khadijah deserves all the pain and regret she feels. The opportunity to reconcile and work things out with me were both on the table, only she chose to refuse them.

I keep up semiregular contact with a few members of her family, either through text message or on social media—only those I trust.

When it's appropriate, I update them on what's happening in Mati's life, but I would be lying if I said I am ready to have them any closer than arm's distance. As fed up with Khadijah's antics as they all were, I still understand deeply that the bonds of family are sacred.

The last news I heard from Khadijah's sister, she had given birth to a second child with her husband. Although I could not muster any happiness for her, a curious fact dawned on me: Mati has half-siblings that someday he will likely be curious about meeting. What will that reunion be like? What will they share with each other? Our life is too good, and our joy has been too hard earned to spend more than a second in worry.

My son knows about his mother. He is made aware of her situation, at least as much as I am able to explain to him. He knows about our ordeal and what happened to him. We talk about our experiences all the time. In the absence of changing our unfortunate past, I'm choosing to be open with him. Better to answer those questions now than try and explain things later on.

We easily forget sometimes that what parents do to one another in their quest for the upper hand, they also do to their children. We are far more aware of how to deal with what happened to us as adults. Children need a little more help moving through their mourning. I try to imbue him with a sense of patience. This can be quite difficult to impart on a child, though.

Turns out, Mati is a well-adjusted kid. This is a quality that goes quite a long way. I am thankful every day that somehow through the chaos he managed to inherit this trait.

When I show Mati the pictures of our escape, from the plane out of Chittagong, and over ice cream in the Dubai airport, he recognizes his younger self. He sees the happiness on my face, too, and remembers our shared relief when the wheels lifted off the ground.

Passive aggression continues out of Khadijah's camp. She holds her son's passports hostage. She refuses to pay her court-ordered costs. As always, a sense of chaos swirls around her every move.

After years of saying as much, the truth has finally sunk in and become hard reality. Nothing that happens with Khadijah surprises me . . . nothing except perhaps doing the right thing.

Should that day come, I won't be around to see it. I have long since ceased waiting for the apology or the olive branch that I know will never come.

My hope is that when Mati grows up and becomes a young man old enough to make his own life choices, he will want to meet and reconnect with his Bangladeshi family. Perhaps by that time, Khadijah will be forced to answer to her son as I have had to all these years.

If Mati ever has that need, my hope for his sake is that she is capable of meeting it.

Whether or not that comes true is out of my control. That's an ongoing lesson from this experience. Only worry about what you can control. The rest isn't worth your time.

• • •

First anniversaries have a way of sneaking up out of the blue. Our first summer together as a family wore to its inevitable end, and October loomed on the horizon. That Halloween night would mark the one-year anniversary since Mati and I arrived home to Naples from Bangladesh.

The adrenaline from our ordeal blurred the first winter months we were back at home. Relief followed as we settled in, after which I had to get my life and business in order.

With our one-year anniversary coming in October, as significant an occasion as we would ever mark as father and son, I felt Mati and I needed to celebrate. And it needed to be memorable.

Zahid and I had spoken quite a few times since our return to Naples. When I called him after landing safely in Dubai that morning, I remember that I put the phone in Mati's hands so Zahid could hear his voice. I wanted him to know it was real.

I kept in touch with him as consistently as I could throughout the year. I offered him a few updates and many tearful thanks, but we had not sat face-to-face since our future hung precariously in doubt in the Chittagong airport parking lot. Although I remembered it as though it happened yesterday, it seemed that a lifetime had already passed.

That was too much time for friends like we had become, I thought. So I called Zahid up and invited him to come to Naples and celebrate our one-year anniversary with us.

Zahid and his partner Tipu had never been to the United States before, which may have been why they acted so surprised when I told them my plan for the celebration.

When Zahid agreed to visit, I could hardly contain my excitement. My friend and I would see one another once again. We would be like two brothers, finally reunited.

Excitement filled me as the days crept closer to our anniversary date. No matter how hard I tried, I could not help but associate where we had been one year before. The memories were still so fresh and vivid.

Zahid and Tipu arrived in Florida on the afternoon of October 11, 2015. One year prior, Mati and I had been estranged, fighting our way in the dark through the complicated Bangladeshi legal system. We had been in a struggle for our life, but now, out on the other side, we were greeting our savior like an old friend. The transformation felt complete.

Mati was happy to see his old friend. My mom and dad were in awe of this man who had been so instrumental in reuniting our family. Again when Zahid and I greeted one another, we embraced like brothers who had been separated by oceans of time. We both agreed that it had been too long.

At first glance, our guests were wide-eyed at Naples' pristine beauty. I could remember telling Zahid about where I came from to pass the time on a few of those bleak nights we spent together back in Dhaka. Now this paradise was a reality to him and his partner, too, something they could see out of their car window, air they could breathe as they took in the spectacular views.

I set up Zahid and Tipu in one of the luxury hotels in downtown Naples. After their first day in town, having just arrived from halfway around the world, they were exhausted. We ate dinner, had a few drinks and laughs, and then said a heartfelt good night.

What I did not tell Zahid that night, what I had managed to keep under my hat amid all of the reunion excitement, was an idea I had concocted over the last few weeks. I wanted to tell our story. No, I had grown in the realization that I needed to tell it.

What I had been through, what Mati had endured at a tender age: our route to becoming a family was both a cautionary tale and an inspirational one. I had recognized for some time that this story had to be told.

Zahid and Tipu spent the next day with my family. Now well rested, everyone was in high spirits. We explored more of Naples, then spent some relaxing time on the beach. Mati showed Zahid his school. We drove around, taking in all the sights. Our tour was a whirlwind.

At the end of the day, Mati and my parents said good-bye and went home for the night. By now, everyone was buzzing, brimming over with excitement.

Zahid, Tipu, and I stayed out. We went to one of the local clubs and ordered a few rounds of drinks. They smoked cigarettes and loosened up further.

I had recognized throughout the day that this reunion was cathartic for Zahid as well as for my family. Somehow, this experience completed a circle for him, too.

After a couple of drinks, we moved to a quieter bar. When the moment was right, I leaned into Zahid. Until then, I had said nothing about my idea to write a book about my ordeal. Although I was not nervous to bring the idea up, I still had no idea what he would feel about my story becoming something more than just some crazy experiences we shared.

"Zahid," I said, finding a moment between sips of drinks and cigarette puffs.

"Yes, Tyler," he replied.

"I have an idea," I said.

As though cued by many months of bouncing one idea or another off of one another, he got excited and leaned in toward me.

"Yes?"

"I want to tell this story," I said. "I want to tell what happened to Mati and me."

His face softened. His eyes went from excitement to warm sincerity. From a broad smile, he motioned gently with his hand, urging me to continue.

Slowly, I reached into my pocket. A smile broke across my face as I laid my iPhone out on the table between us and pressed record.

"Go ahead," I said. "Tell me how you saw the whole ordeal."

ABOUT THE AUTHOR

• • •

TYLER WOOD IS THE SENIOR vice president of global business development for Mediatrix Capital. He specializes in algorithmic currency trading and artificial intelligence and also consults private clients in hedge fund formation and the construction of alternative investment portfolios.

Wood traveled extensively for his international business education. He studied in China, France, India, Japan, Malaysia, New Zealand, Panama, Singapore, and South Africa. His passion for philanthropy led to his ten-year relationship with Kiva.org, a nonprofit microlending organization.

Before all these roles, however, Wood is a devoted and loving father to his son, Mati Wood.

Made in the USA
Middletown, DE
20 May 2017